THE OBJECT-Z SPECIFICATION LANGUAGE

Advances in Formal Methods

Series Editor

Michael Hinchey

THE OBJECT-Z SPECIFICATION LANGUAGE

by

Graeme Smith
University of Queensland, Australia

KLUWER ACADEMIC PUBLISHERS
Boston / Dordrecht / London

Distributors for North, Central and South America:
Kluwer Academic Publishers
101 Philip Drive
Assinippi Park
Norwell, Massachusetts 02061 USA
Telephone (781) 871-6600
Fax (781) 871-6528
E-Mail <kluwer@wkap.com>

Distributors for all other countries:
Kluwer Academic Publishers Group
Distribution Centre
Post Office Box 322
3300 AH Dordrecht, THE NETHERLANDS
Telephone 31 78 6392 392
Fax 31 78 6546 474
E-Mail <orderdept@wkap.nl>

Electronic Services <http://www.wkap.nl>

Library of Congress Cataloging-in-Publication Data

Smith, Graeme, 1966-
The Object-Z specification language / by Graeme Smith.
p. cm. -- (Advances in formal methods ; 1)
Includes bibliographical references and index.
ISBN 0-7923-8684-1 (alk. paper)
1. Object-oriented programming (Computer science) 2. Z (Computer program language) I. Title. II. Series.

QA76.64 S579 1999
005.1'17--dc21

99-047408

Printed on acid-free paper.

Printed in the United States of America

Series Forward
Advances in Formal Methods

Series Editor

Michael Hinchey

University of Nebraska-Omaha
College of Information Science and Technology
Department of Computer Science
Omaha, NE 68182-0500 USA

Email: mhinchey@unomaha.edu

As early as 1949, computer pioneers realized that writing a program that executed as planned was no simple task. Turing even saw the need to address the issues of program correctness and termination, foretelling groundbreaking work of Edsger Dijkstra, John McCarthy, Bob Floyd, Tony Hoare, Sue Owicki and David Gries, among others, two and three decades later.

The term *formal methods* refers to the application of mathematical techniques for the specification, analysis, design, implementation and subsequent maintenance of complex computer software and hardware. These techniques have proven themselves, when correctly and appropriately applied, to result in systems of the highest quality, which are well documented, easier to maintain, and promote software reuse.

With emerging legislation, and increasing emphasis in standards and university curricula, formal methods are set to become even more important in system development. This Kluwer book series, Advances in Formal Methods, aims to present results from the cutting edge of formal methods research and practice.

Books in the series will address the use of formal methods in both hardware and software development, and the role of formal methods in the development of safety-critical and real-time systems, hardware-software co-design, testing, simulation and prototyping, software quality assurance, software reuse, security, and many other areas. The series aims to include both basic and advanced textbooks, monographs, reference books and collections of high quality papers which will address managerial issues, the development process, requirements engineering, tool support, methods integration, metrics, reverse engineering, and issues relating to formal methods education.

It is our aim that, in due course, Advances in Formal Methods will provide a rich source of information for students, teachers, academic researchers and industrial practitioners alike. And I hope that, for many, it will be a first port-of-call for relevant texts and literature.

This book is a particularly welcome addition to the series. It represents the first widely-available full and authoritative reference to Object-Z. Object-Z enriches Z, the most widely used formal specification notation, with object-oriented primitives that facilitate the specification (and ultimately the implementation) of object-based systems. Graeme Smith, as one of the contributors to much of the development of Object-Z and a world-class researcher, is a leading authority on the language and has written what I expect will become an indispensable aid to anyone planning to use Object-Z.

Professor Mike Hinchey

To Lisa

Contents

Preface

The Object-Z specification language came into existence in late 1988 as part of a collaborative project between the Department of Computer Science at the University of Queensland and the Overseas Telecommunications Corporation (OTC) of Australia. A primary motivation was the need to enhance structuring in the Z specification language (on which Object-Z is based) in order to more effectively specify medium- to large-scale software systems. A more fundamental motivation was the desire to investigate the integration of formal techniques with the methodology of object orientation: a methodology which at that time was gaining rapid popularity in the programming community.

The development of Object-Z continued at the University of Queensland culminating in 1991 with a technical report entitled *The Object-Z Specification Language: Version 1* which provided a complete description of the language including a full concrete syntax and several illustrative case studies. This document quickly became the de facto standard for Object-Z as its popularity increased both at the University of Queensland and in other universities and research institutes throughout the world.

Now, several years on, the popularity of Object-Z is still growing. However, the language has undergone major changes and reached a new level of maturity with the existence of axiomatic and denotational semantics and the first tools. It is for this reason that a new standard is now needed. This book aims to provide this standard by presenting a comprehensive description of the language in terms of informal and semi-formal descriptions of all language constructs, type rules, specification guidelines and a full formal syntax. Its format has been inspired by J.M. Spivey's highly successful *The Z Notation* (Prentice Hall, 1989 & 1992) and the use of "manual pages" to enable easy access to definitions of constructs has been adopted. For reasons of conciseness and avoiding reiteration, a knowledge of Z is assumed throughout this book and only those constructs particular to Object-Z are addressed in detail. For readers unfamiliar with Z, I highly recommend first reading Spivey's book or one of the other excellent textbooks available on the Z notation.

This book is aimed at people requiring a deep understanding of the Object-Z language: system developers, researchers and postgraduate students. It would also be a valuable aid, however, to lecturers wishing to teach Object-Z in undergraduate courses or, simply, to anyone wanting to learn or use Object-Z. The following chapter summary will help you get the most from this book.

Chapter 1 — Introduction
This chapter motivates and introduces the Object-Z language. It begins with a section outlining some of the benefits of adopting an object-oriented approach to formal specification and then introduces the major object-oriented constructs of Object-Z via the specification of simple data structures. The use of these constructs is then further illustrated by a small case study.

Chapter 2 — Semantic Basis
This chapter informally describes the basis of the semantics of Object-Z. This semantics is in terms of object identities, which act as references in much the same way as pointers in a programming language. The consequences of adopting such a semantics on both system design and the related notions of modularity and compositionality are discussed.

Chapter 3 — Syntactic Constructs
This chapter provides an informal definition of each of the syntactic constructs in Object-Z which are not also in Z. Scope rules and the usage of the constructs is detailed. The chapter's goal is to assist the understanding of the more rigorous descriptions of Object-Z in Chapters 4 and 6.

Chapter 4 — Language Definition
This chapter has a "manual page" for each of the syntactic constructs introduced in Chapter 3 comprising the name of the construct, its formal syntax, a brief description of the construct in English text, its rules of usage including type rules (also in English text) and a semi-formal definition using a simple meta-language. The meta-language, introduced at the beginning of the chapter, allows the meaning of Object-Z constructs to be expressed in terms of constructs of Z.

Chapter 5 — Concurrent Systems
This chapter presents guidelines for specifying concurrent systems comprising arbitrary and variable sized collections of similar components in Object-Z. Techniques for specifying aggregation, synchronization, communication and nondeterminism are introduced by simple examples. The use of these techniques is then further illustrated by a small case study.

Chapter 6 — Concrete Syntax
This chapter presents the full concrete syntax of Object-Z including operator precedences.

Since a number of definitions of both Z and Object-Z have appeared over the years, it is prudent to say a word about their relationship to this book. The language presented in this book is based on Z as defined in the second edition of J.M. Spivey's *The Z Notation* (Prentice Hall, 1992). All other definitions of Z are only consistent with the language in this book insofar as they are consistent with Spivey.

The major difference with other recent definitions of Object-Z is the omission, in this book, of history invariants. The reason for this is the instability of their definition. They are not included in the existing axiomatic and denotational semantics of the language and not supported by the Wizard type checker. Rather than excluding them from Object-Z, however, the aim of this book is to provide a standard for Object-Z to which history invariants, and possibly other constructs, can eventually be added.

Acknowledgements

I would like to thank Gordon Rose, Clemens Fischer and Sam Valentine for their detailed comments on earlier drafts of this book.

Object-Z has been developed over a number of years by a changing team of researchers and postgraduate students. It is the work of this team rather than any individual which is presented in this book.

First and foremost, I must acknowledge the contributions of Roger Duke and Gordon Rose who have led the development of Object-Z since its beginning. Their deep insights and stimulating discussions have inspired most, if not all, of the significant developments in the language. The following people must also be acknowledged for their invaluable contributions to Object-Z — David Carrington, Jin Song Dong, David Duke, Alena Griffiths, Paul King and Wendy Johnston.

Finally, I wish to acknowledge everyone, from student to visiting lecturer, who has attended the Formal Methods Group meetings at the University of Queensland over the last 10 years. By bringing along fresh perspectives and new ideas, they too have contributed greatly to the Object-Z specification language presented in this book.

Brisbane, Australia Graeme Smith
July, 1999

1

Introduction

If I were writing a paper, or preparing slides for a lecture, and required a concise, yet readable, definition of Object-Z, I would probably write something like this:

> Object-Z is an extension of Z to facilitate specification in an object-oriented style.

The first thing which should catch the reader's eye is the word "extension". This captures the notion that Object-Z is based on another language, namely Z, and that rather than modifying or adapting its definition, Object-Z extends it. In fact, Object-Z is a conservative extension of Z in the sense that all Z's syntax and its associated semantics are also part of Object-Z. Therefore, any Z specification is also an Object-Z specification.

The next important word in this definition is "facilitate". This word is purposely chosen to reflect the fact that Object-Z doesn't enforce any particular style of specification. Indeed, we have just seen that any Z specification is also an Object-Z specification. Object-Z does, however, extend Z with constructs which help the specifier, if he or she wishes, to specify systems in a particular fashion.

A hint as to what these constructs might be is given by the final key word in the definition — "object-oriented". This should bring to mind notions of classes and objects, inheritance and polymorphism.

We begin this chapter by looking at the motivation behind Object-Z. We do not discuss the benefits of formal methods, nor those of object orientation — this has been done elsewhere. Instead, we examine some of the benefits of combining the methodology of object orientation with formal methods.

The Object-Z language is then introduced through the specification of simple data structures which allow us to compare Object-Z with Z and to illustrate the major object-oriented constructs. The use of these constructs is then illustrated further by the specification of a small case study — a simplified version of the game of Tetris.

To introduce Object-Z completely, I would, of course, also need to introduce the Z notation. However, there are a number of excellent books on Z already available — a selection of these are listed in the bibliography — and I am certain I could not improve on them. Therefore, I assume the reader has a sufficient background knowledge of Z and confine my discussions in this chapter, as in the rest of the book, to those constructs particular to Object-Z.

1.1 Motivation

Object orientation — see the bibliography for references — is a modular design methodology based on the notion that a system is composed of a collection of interacting objects. The behaviour of an object is determined by its *class*: a mechanism for encapsulating an object's state with the set of operations it may undergo. Each class generally defines more than one object in a system and may also be reused in the definition of other classes. The latter is achieved by a method of incremental modification of classes known as *inheritance*. The classes which inherit a given class are known as its subclasses and, through inheritance, are often in some way compatible with it. Hence it can be useful that an object belong, rather than to a particular class, to a given class or any one of its subclasses. This notion is referred to as *polymorphism*.

Object orientation emerged as a major programming paradigm due to the need to handle complexity in large-scale software systems. It helped fulfill this need through a combination of sound modular design and software reusability. In the same way, object orientation can solve some of the scalability problems of formal methods. Also, by providing a common methodology, object orientation can help bridge the gap between the specification and implementation of software systems.

Modularity

Most of the benefits of object orientation stem from the modularity it brings to system design. Modularity increases the clarity of specifications by allowing a reader to focus on one part at a time. In a Z specification, for example, to deduce in which ways a particular state variable may change, the reader must search the entire specification for any reference to the state schema of that variable in an operation schema. In large specifications, this becomes impracticable without appropriate tools or some informal organization of the schemas within the specification.

A fundamental idea of object orientation, however, is that the state of an object may be changed only by the operations of its class. Hence by adopting the notion of class in Z, the relationship between state and operation schemas can be made explicit. In general, the reader of an object-oriented specification can concentrate on one class at a time in isolation from the rest of the specification and then, when he or she is familiar with each class, examine how objects of those classes are arranged to form the specified system.

The reuse of classes via inheritance also improves readability by allowing the reader to use his or her knowledge of existing classes (possibly from a class library) to understand a given class. Inheritance also aids the writer of the specification who can specify classes by drawing on similarities with existing classes and, by so doing, avoid repeatedly specifying common class structures.

The modularity provided by classes, as well as helping in the specification stage of a formal development, can also help in subsequent stages of verification and refinement. Once again, this is achieved by allowing the system developer to focus on one part of the specification at a time.

The classes of a specification define the behaviours of the objects of the specified system. Therefore, behavioural properties of these objects can be deduced from their classes in isolation. These properties can then be used, taking into account the system structure, to prove properties of the overall system. Such a compositional approach to verification can greatly reduce the complexity of proofs.

Similarly, a compositional approach can be taken to refinement. A system specification can be refined by refining the classes of the specification in isolation. Since the objects of the refined classes will only behave in ways which the objects of the original classes could have behaved, the entire system will also only behave in a way which the original system could have behaved.

Methodology

Another benefit of object orientation is that it provides a precise methodology for system design. This methodology involves the specification of a system by first specifying the behaviour of its constituent objects by classes, and by utilizing inheritance and polymorphism where appropriate. It has been applied extensively in the analysis, design and implementation of software systems providing the specifier with a wide range of experience to draw upon.

Having a methodology guides the specifier in the style in which the specification is presented. Z offers no such methodology allowing specifications in many different styles. Although this gives the specifier more flexibility, it also presents him or her with an extra task when beginning a new specification: deciding upon an approach or strategy for structuring the specification. This decision is not always easy, especially for a novice, and is often only reached by a process of trial and error.

This lack of methodology in Z, also presents the reader of the specification with the task of becoming familiar with the specification structure. In general, this will need to be done before the specification itself can be read. With an object-oriented specification, on the other hand, the reader is aware in advance of the approach the specifier has taken and is consequently better prepared to read the specification.

"Seamless" development

The final benefit of object orientation we are going to discuss is that of "seamless" development. What this means is the use of common concepts and system structuring at each stage of system development: from the specification right through to the implementation. This is possible when using an object-oriented approach to specification and then implementing in an object-oriented programming language. It makes the specification more accessible to the programmer, who may not be a formalist, and facilitates his or her task of transforming the specification to implementation.

In fact, the specification can be refined to represent the exact structure of the implementation; so that there is a direct mapping, not only between classes, but also between each operation, in the specification and those in the actual software. This encourages a fully formal approach to the final refinement from specification to code and, in the case of a rigorous, as opposed to formal, approach, reduces the chance of error.

1.2 Classes

The remainder of this chapter introduces the Object-Z specification language by the specification of simple data structures which could be used in the specification of a larger system, and a small case study. As a preliminary, and in order to compare Object-Z with Z, we start by specifying a generic queue in standard Z.

The state of the queue comprises a variable *items* denoting the items in the queue and a variable *count* which records the total number of items which have ever joined the queue. The latter could be used for statistical reasons, for example, in the system in which the queue is used. The state is modelled by the state schema $Queue[Item]$ — the formal generic parameter *Item* is the type of the items in the queue.

$$
\begin{array}{|l}
\hline
Queue[Item] \\
\hline
items : \mathrm{seq}\ Item \\
count : \mathbb{N} \\
\hline
\end{array}
$$

Initially, the queue is empty and no items have been joined to the queue. This is modelled by the schema $QueueInit[Item]$.

$$
\begin{array}{|l}
\hline
QueueInit[Item] \\
\hline
Queue[Item] \\
\hline
items = \langle\rangle \\
count = 0 \\
\hline
\end{array}
$$

Items may join and leave the queue on a first-in/first-out basis. The operation schema $Join[Item]$ models the join operation. The item to be joined to the queue is input as the variable $item?$ and is appended to the state variable *items*. The state variable *count* is incremented.

$$
\begin{array}{|l}
\hline
Join[Item] \\
\hline
\Delta Queue[Item] \\
item? : Item \\
\hline
items' = items \frown \langle item? \rangle \\
count' = count + 1 \\
\hline
\end{array}
$$

The operation $Leave[Item]$ models the leave operation. The head of *items* is removed and output as variable $item!$. The state variable *count* is unchanged.

$$
\begin{array}{|l}
\hline
Leave[Item] \\
\hline
\Delta Queue[Item] \\
item! : Item \\
\hline
items = \langle item! \rangle \frown items' \\
count' = count \\
\hline
\end{array}
$$

Let us now consider specifying the same queue as a class in Object-Z. Object-Z classes introduce, as well as modularity, a precise notion of interface. The interface of a class defines the ways in which objects of that class interact with their environment. It determines the ways in which objects of the class can be used in a system specification. More precisely, it defines which state variables may be accessed, whether initial conditions can be checked, and which operations may be applied.

Z has no formal notion of interface. Usually, to allow for data refinement, it is assumed that only the initial state schema and operations, and not the state variables, of a specification are accessible in its environment. However, often a Z specification will include auxiliary operation schemas, which are not themselves operations of the specification, but used to build such operations. Such auxiliary operation schemas are not intended to be part of the specification's interface but are not formally distinguished from those operation schemas that are.

In Object-Z, the notion of interface is made precise by the inclusion in a class of a *visibility list*. Let us assume that the interface of the queue comprises the state variable $count$, the initial state schema and the operations $Join$ and $Leave$ only. That is, the state variable $items$ of a queue object represents internal information which cannot be accessed in the system which contains that object. The queue is modelled by the class $Queue[Item]$.

$$
\begin{array}{l}
\textbf{class } Queue[Item] \\
\quad \upharpoonright (count, \mathrm{INIT}, Join, Leave) \\
\quad \hline \\
\quad items : \mathrm{seq}\ Item \\
\quad count : \mathbb{N} \\
\quad \hline \\
\quad \mathrm{INIT} \\
\quad items = \langle\,\rangle \\
\quad count = 0 \\
\quad \hline \\
\quad Join \\
\quad \Delta(items, count) \\
\quad item? : Item \\
\quad \hline \\
\quad items' = items \frown \langle item? \rangle \\
\quad count' = count + 1 \\
\quad \hline \\
\quad Leave \\
\quad \Delta(items) \\
\quad item! : Item \\
\quad \hline \\
\quad items = \langle item! \rangle \frown items'
\end{array}
$$

The class is generic with the formal generic parameter *Item* representing, as in the Z specification, the type of the items in the queue. The scope of this parameter is the entire class. Hence, unlike in the Z specification, there is no need to introduce the formal generic parameter to each schema definition.

The first construct in the class is the visibility list. It specifies that the state variable $count$, the initial state schema and the operations $Join$ and $Leave$ are in the class's interface. In general, the visibility list of a class explicitly lists those *features* — constants (introduced in Section 1.4), state variables, initial state schema and operations — of a class which are in the class's interface and, hence, "visible" to the environment of objects of the class. When all such features are in a class's interface then the visibility list is not required. That is, the absence of a visibility list implies all features are visible.

Unlike in Z where the roles of schemas as modelling the state, initial state or operations of a system are indicated only by informal conventions, the role of each schema in an Object-Z class is formally indicated by its header. The first schema of the class $Queue[T]$ is the state schema. Its role as state schema is distinguished by the fact that it has no name associated with it. The body of the schema is identical to that in the Z specification. In general, state schemas are not like standard Z schemas since they may have their declarations partitioned according to the roles of the declared variables. This is explained further in Section 1.3.

The second schema of the class is the initial state schema — indicated by the name *INIT*. This name is a reserved word which cannot be used for any other purpose in a specification. Since the initial state schema of a class can only refer to one state schema — that which is encapsulated with it in the class — rather than requiring the specifier to include the state schema in the initial state schema's definition, it is, instead, implicitly included. Hence, the initial state schema of $Queue[T]$ refers to the state variables $items$ and $count$ even though these are not included explicitly in a declaration. In fact, an initial state schema never includes declarations. It simply models a condition which holds initially and this condition is specified entirely by its predicate.

All schemas in a class, apart from those distinguished as the state and initial state schemas, are operations. Again the state schema is implicitly included in any operation. Furthermore, the state schema in primed form is also implicitly included. That is, the operations of class $Queue[T]$ can refer to the variables $items$, $count$, $items'$ and $count'$.

A class operation extends the notion of a standard Z schema by adding to it a Δ-list (read "delta-list"). The Δ-list is a list of state variables which may be changed by the operation. In other words, all state variables not in the Δ-list remain unchanged. The operation $Join$ of class $Queue[T]$ changes both the state variables $items$ and $count$, whereas the operation $Leave$ changes only $items$. Therefore, it is not necessary to include the predicate $count' = count$ in $Leave$ as in the Z specification. In general, the primed form of a variable appearing in an operation's Δ-list need not be constrained by the predicate of the operation allowing variables to be changed nondeterministically.

As this example shows, the Object-Z class notation can simplify the schema definitions of even the most basic of Z specifications. The true power of classes is only seen, however, when they are used to define systems of interacting objects. An example of this is provided in Section 1.3.

1.3 Objects

Although classes in Object-Z can be used to specify entire systems, they are more often used to specify components of systems. The components of these systems are not the classes themselves, but objects of the classes. An object is an instance of a class in the sense that it can only be used according to the class's interface and that its behaviour is consistent with that defined by the schemas of the class.

Consider specifying a simple multiplexer which comprises three components: two input queues and a single output queue of messages. The messages on the input queues are merged onto the output queue. The multiplexer is either *idle*, when both input queues are empty, or *busy*, otherwise.

The multiplexer is also specified by a class — a *system class*. Let its interface comprise a variable *status* denoting the status of the multiplexer, its initial state schema, operations $Join_1$, modelling the joining of a message onto one of the input queues, and $Join_2$, modelling the joining of a message onto the other, an operation *Transfer* modelling the transfer of a message from an input to the output queue, and an operation *Leave* modelling a message leaving the output queue.

The type of the messages and the type of the variable *status* are provided by the following basic type and free type definition.

$$[Message]$$
$$Status ::= idle \mid busy$$

The multiplexer is specified by the class *Multiplexer*.

Multiplexer

$$\restriction(status, \mathrm{INIT}, Join_1, Join_2, Transfer, Leave)$$

$$input_1, input_2, output : Queue[Message]$$
$$source : Queue[Queue[Message]]$$
$$\Delta$$
$$status : Status$$

$$input_1 \neq input_2 \land input_1 \neq output \land input_2 \neq output$$
$$status = idle \Leftrightarrow output.count = input_1.count + input_2.count$$

INIT

$$input_1.\mathrm{INIT} \land input_2.\mathrm{INIT} \land output.\mathrm{INIT} \land source.\mathrm{INIT}$$

$$Join_1 \mathrel{\widehat=} input_1.Join$$
$$Join_2 \mathrel{\widehat=} input_2.Join$$
$$Leave_1 \mathrel{\widehat=} input_1.Leave \land source.Join[input_1/item?]$$
$$Leave_2 \mathrel{\widehat=} input_2.Leave \land source.Join[input_2/item?]$$
$$Transfer \mathrel{\widehat=} (Leave_1 \mathbin{[\,]} Leave_2) \parallel output.Join$$
$$Leave \mathrel{\widehat=} output.Leave \land source.Leave$$

The state schema of this class has its variables partitioned by a Δ into *primary* and *secondary* variables. The primary variables, above the Δ, are like the variables of class $Queue[Item]$: they may only be changed by an operation which explicitly includes them in its Δ-list. Secondary variables, below the Δ, however, are implicitly available for change in any operation. Usually the value of a secondary variable is uniquely defined in terms of the values of one or more primary variables. Hence, it only changes to maintain its relationship with those primary variables.

The primary variables $input_1$, $input_2$ and $output$ are of type $Queue[Message]$ — the class $Queue[Item]$ with its generic parameter instantiated with the type $Message$. When a class is used as a type, it denotes a set of *object identities*. These uniquely identify objects of that class. Therefore, $input_1$, $input_2$ and $output$ are identities of objects of class $Queue[Message]$. The first predicate of the state schema ensures that these identities are in fact distinct — that is, that the primary variables identify different objects.

Similarly, the primary variable $source$ is the identity of a queue object whose items are object identities of $Queue[Message]$. Its purpose is to record from which input queue — $queue_1$ or $queue_2$ — each message in $output$ originated.

The secondary variable $status$ models the multiplexer's status. Its value is uniquely defined by the second predicate of the state schema. This predicate uses a dot notation to refer to the values of the $count$ variables of queue objects identified by the primary variables. The variable $status$ is idle if, and only if, the $count$ variable of the object identified by $output$ is equal to the sum of the $count$ variables of the objects identified by $input_1$ and $input_2$. In other words, the multiplexer is idle whenever the number of messages joined to the output queue is equal to the total number of messages joined to the input queues. In general, the dot notation can be used in this way to refer to any visible *attribute* — constant or state variable — of a class.

The dot notation is also used to specify that an object is in its initial state and to specify that an object undergoes an operation. The former is only possible when INIT is in the visibility list of the object's class and is illustrated by the initial state schema of $Multiplexer$. This schema states that each of the queue objects identified by the primary variables are in their initial states. That is, each identified queue object contains no messages and its $count$ variable is equal to zero.

The application of operations to objects is also only possible when the operations are visible. The operations $Join_1$ and $Join_2$ model a message being joined to the queue objects identified by $input_1$ and $input_2$ respectively. The input and output variables of these operations are those of the $Join$ operation of class $Queue[Message]$. That is, the operations have a single input variable $item?$ of type $Message$.

These operations do not change any primary variables of the class. Although the object identified by either $input_1$ or $input_2$ is changed — a message is joined to it — the object's identity is not. This distinction between an object and its identity is central to Object-Z and is discussed in detail in Chapter 2. The secondary state variable $status$ will be changed by either operation if it is $idle$ before the operation.

The remaining operations of $Multiplexer$ utilize, as well as the dot notation, *operation operators*. These are analogous to the schema operators of Z and enable the specification of more complex operations.

The conjunction operator $\wedge$ used in operations $Leave_1$, $Leave_2$ and *Leave* enables the specification of the simultaneous occurrence of operations. It conjoins its argument operations and is similar to the schema conjunction operator, also $\wedge$, of Z.

The operation $Leave_1$ models a message leaving the queue object identified by $input_1$ and the identity of this queue object being joined to the queue object identified by *source*. The latter is achieved by renaming the input *item*? of *source.Join* to $input_1$. Similarly, the operation $Leave_2$ models a message leaving the queue object identified by $input_2$ and the identity of this queue object being joined to the queue object identified by *source*. Since $Leave_1$ and $Leave_2$ are not in the class's interface, they cannot be applied to an object of class *Multiplexer*. They are used, however, in the definition of the visible operation *Transfer*.

The operation *Leave* models a message leaving the queue object identified by *output* and the identity of the input queue from which the message originated leaving the queue object identified by *source*.

The operation *Transfer* utilizes two operation operators. The parallel composition operator $\|$ enables the specification of inter-object communication. Its argument operations are conjoined and communication between them is achieved by equating inputs of one with outputs of the other whenever the basenames of these inputs and outputs are the same — that is, whenever the names of the inputs and outputs are the same apart from the ? or ! decorations. The equated inputs and outputs are then hidden in the resulting operation. The operator is similar to the piping operator $\gg$ of Z except that it allows communication in both directions.

The operation *Transfer* models a message leaving one of the queue objects identified by $input_1$ and $input_2$, and joining the queue object identified by *output*. The transfer of the message is achieved due to the output variable *item*! of $Leave_1$ and $Leave_2$ having the same basename (*item*) as the input variable *item*? of *output.Join*.

The choice of input queue is modelled in *Transfer* using the nondeterministic choice operator $[]$. This operator is used to model *angelic choice* between operations. That is, the choice depends on which of the operations are enabled. When only one of the operations is enabled then this operation will be chosen and applied. When both of the operations are enabled, a nondeterministic choice is made between either one operation, the other operation or both of the operations being applied. The operator is similar to the schema disjunction operator $\vee$ of Z.

In *Transfer*, the operator provides an example of modelling the internal behaviour of objects. Although the occurrence of the *Transfer* operation can be controlled by the environment of a multiplexer object, the choice of which input queue to transfer a message from when both are non-empty is controlled only by the object itself.

Objects of class *Multiplexer* can, of course, be used in further system classes as can those system classes themselves. This process can continue indefinitely, resulting in highly structured specifications of systems which can be understood in terms of their simpler components. An understanding of the behaviour of these systems, however, needs to account for the possibility of *object aliasing*. Aliasing occurs when two or more variables in the specification identify the same object. *Multiplexer* is free of aliasing since the queue objects are distinct. This is not always the case and, indeed, not always desired. The issues of aliasing will be discussed in more detail in Chapter 2.

1.4 Inheritance

As well as being used to specify objects, Object-Z classes can be directly reused in the definition of other classes. A class may be specified as a specialization or extension of another class using inheritance. The inheriting class, or *subclass*, implicitly includes all of the features of the inherited class, or *superclass*, and may also modify and add to these features.

As an example of specialization of a class through inheritance, consider specifying a bounded queue. Such a queue can only contain up to a fixed number of items. Therefore, after this number of items have been joined to the queue, an item must leave before further items can be joined. The bounded queue is modelled by the class $BoundedQueue[Item]$.

$BoundedQueue[Item]$

$\upharpoonright(count, \text{I}{\small NIT}, Join, Leave)$

$Queue[Item]$

$max : \mathbb{N}$

$\#items \leqslant max$

$Join$

$\#items < max$

When a class inherits another, only the features — variables, constants, initial state schema and operations — are inherited; the visibility list is not. Therefore, it is necessary to specify the visibility list of the subclass. This enables visible features of the superclass to be removed from the subclass's interface, and features of the superclass not in its interface to be visible in the subclass.

The class $BoundedQueue[Item]$ inherits $Queue[Item]$ maintaining the same interface. It adds to the features of $Queue[Item]$, however, a constant max denoting the maximum number of items the queue can contain. Constants are specified in Object-Z classes by axiomatic definitions in the same way global constants are specified in Z. Their scope, however, is limited to the class in which they are declared. A constant is associated with a fixed value which, unlike the values of state variables, cannot be changed by any operation of the class. This value may, however, differ for different objects of the class.

The inherited state schema of $Queue[Item]$ is extended with a predicate stating that the number of items in the queue is less than or equal to max. The explicitly specified state schema in $BoundedQueue[Item]$ is conjoined with that inherited from $Queue[Item]$. Similarly, an explicitly declared initial state schema would be conjoined with the inherited initial state schema and any explicitly declared operation would be conjoined with an identically named inherited operation.

The predicate added to the inherited state schema is implicitly included in the inherited initial state schema and precondition and postcondition of each inherited operation. Hence, it alone is all that is needed to specify the bounded queue. However, for clarity, a precondition is also added to the operation *Join* which states that the number of items in the queue is less than max.

The class $BoundedQueue[Item]$ is equivalent to the following class specified without using inheritance.

$BoundedQueue[Item]$

$\upharpoonright(count, \mathrm{INIT}, Join, Leave)$

$max : \mathbb{N}$

$items : \mathrm{seq}\ Item$
$count : \mathbb{N}$

$\#items \leqslant max$

INIT

$items = \langle\rangle$
$count = 0$

$Join$

$\Delta(items, count)$
$item? : Item$

$\#items < max$
$items' = items \frown \langle item? \rangle$
$count' = count + 1$

$Leave$

$\Delta(items)$
$item! : Item$

$items = \langle item! \rangle \frown items'$

As an example of specifying an extension of a class through inheritance, consider specifying a queue whose *count* variable can be reset to zero. The resettable queue is modelled by the class $ResettableQueue[Item]$.

$ResettableQueue[Item]$

$\upharpoonright(count, \mathrm{INIT}, Join, Leave, Reset)$

$Queue[Item]$

$Reset$

$\Delta(count)$

$count' = 0$

This class also inherits *Queue*[*Item*] but, in this case, extends the interface to include the new operation *Reset*.

The examples of inheritance so far have involved inheriting a single class. However, it is possible for a class to inherit more than one class. The result is identical to inheriting each of the classes individually in an arbitrary order. As an example of such multiple inheritance , consider specifying a bounded queue whose *count* variable can be reset. This queue is modelled by the class *ResettableBoundedQueue*[*Item*].

```
┌─ ResettableBoundedQueue[Item] ──────────────
│ ↾(count, INIT, Join, Leave, Reset)
│ BoundedQueue[Item]
│ ResettableQueue[Item]
└─────────────────────────────────────────────
```

This class inherits *BoundedQueue*[*Item*] and *ResettableQueue*[*Item*] and hence includes the features of both classes. The state schemas of each inherited class are conjoined to form the state schema of *ResettableBoundedQueue*[*Item*]. Similarly, the initial state schemas and operations *Join* and *Leave* are also conjoined to form the initial state schema and operations *Join* and *Leave* respectively of *ResettableBounded-Queue*[*Item*].

Each of the subclasses of *Queue*[*Item*] specified above are behaviourally similar to *Queue*[*Item*] in the sense that they all model queues — items join and leave on a first-in/first-out basis. Inheritance, however, is really just a means of reuse of existing specification text and it is possible to specify subclasses with behaviour unrelated to their superclasses. This can be done through a combination of renaming and cancellation of inherited features. Consider using the class *Queue*[*Item*] to specify a generic stack. Although this is not a particularly intuitive way to model a stack, it highlights the reuse of text through inheritance. Rather than *Join* and *Leave* in the class interface, we require operations *Push* and *Pop* which allow items to be added and removed on a first-in/last-out basis. The stack is modelled by the class *Stack*[*Item*].

```
┌─ Stack[Item] ───────────────────────────────
│ ↾(count, INIT, Push, Pop)
│ Queue[Item][Pop/Leave]
│
│ ┌─ Push ────────────────────────────────────
│ │ Δ(items)
│ │ item? : Item
│ ├──────────
│ │ items' = ⟨item?⟩ ⁀ items
│ └───────────────────────────────────────────
└─────────────────────────────────────────────
```

This class inherits *Queue*[*Item*] with *Leave* renamed to *Pop*. Renaming can be similarly applied to any feature of a class. The operation *Join* is effectively cancelled by its absence from the visibility list. It should be noted, however, that *Join* is still available and could be made visible again in a subclass of *Stack*[*Item*]. The new operation *Push* models the addition of an item to the top of the stack.

1.5 Polymorphism

Although each object of an Object-Z specification belongs to a unique class, it is not always necessary to precisely identify that class. Polymorphism allows an object to be declared as belonging to one class from a particular inheritance hierarchy — a collection of classes comprising a given class and all the classes in the specification which inherit, either directly or indirectly, the features of this class. For expressions involving the object to be well-formed, it is necessary that the interface of each subclass of the hierarchy include all the features of the interface of the given class.

As an example of such an inheritance hierarchy, consider a specification which includes the various queue classes of Section 1.4. This hierarchy is shown in Figure 1.1 where arrows point from subclasses to superclasses. Note that we are assuming the class $Stack[Item]$ is not part of the specification and hence not in the hierarchy.

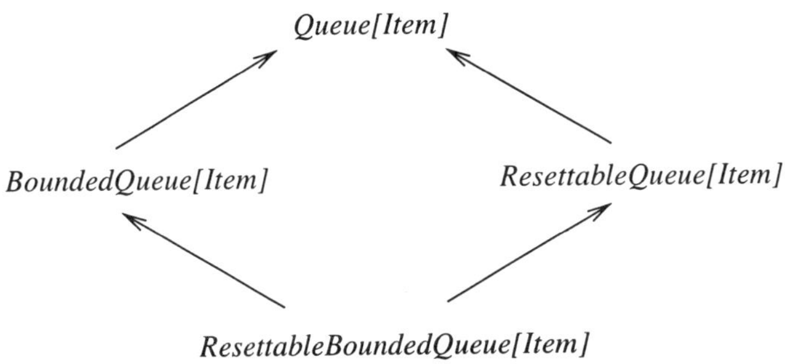

Figure 1.1: Queue hierarchy

Each class in this hierarchy includes in its visibility list the features in the visibility list of $Queue[Item]$ — $count$, $\textsc{Init}$, $Join$ and $Leave$. Therefore, if we require a queue object in a specification and wish to allow the possibility that the queue is bounded or resettable then we can declare it polymorphically as follows.

$$queue : \downarrow Queue[Item]$$

The class of the object identified by the variable $queue$ is of one of those in the inheritance hierarchy of Figure 1.1 — $Queue[Item]$, $BoundedQueue[Item]$, $ResettableQueue[Item]$ or $ResettableBoundedQueue[Item]$. Polymorphism in Object-Z is similar to genericity in the sense that it allows a variable to be declared which can be associated with more than one type. Therefore, as with genericity, we can only use that variable in expressions that a variable of any of its possible types could be used. While the expression $queue.count$ and the operation expressions $queue.Join$ and $queue.Leave$ are well-formed, without further qualification (explained in Chapter 3), the operation expression $queue.Reset$ is not — since the object identified by $queue$ may be of class $Queue[Item]$ or $BoundedQueue[Item]$.

If we wished to be able to reset the queue, we could instead declare it as follows.

$$queue : \downarrow ResettableQueue[Item]$$

The object identified by the variable $queue$, in this case, is of class $ResettableQueue[Item]$ or $ResettableBoundedQueue[Item]$. The accessible features are the visible features of $ResettableQueue[Item]$.

1.6 Case Study: Tetris

In this section, we illustrate the usage of the object-oriented constructs introduced in previous sections by specifying a small case study — a simplified version of the game of Tetris. The game is played by a single player on a computer screen — a typical snapshot is shown in Figure 1.2.

Figure 1.2: Game of Tetris

The goal of the player of Tetris is to position falling blocks of various shapes so that entire rows of the playing screen are filled. When a row is filled, it disappears from the screen, the rows above it move down and the player's score is advanced. The game continues until the fallen blocks pile up to the top of the playing screen.

The blocks fall, one at a time, until they reach either the bottom of the playing screen or another block which has previously fallen. The player positions the falling blocks by moving them left and right and by rotating them. In this simplified version of the game, we will assume blocks can only be rotated in a clockwise direction.

We begin the specification by specifying an abstract class *Grid*. Objects of this class do not appear in the specification. Rather it is used as a basis for defining other classes of the specification by inheritance.

The class *Grid* models a two dimensional grid which may have some of its positions filled. It is used in the specification to define both the playing screen and the various types of blocks of the game.

Grid

$$width, height : \mathbb{N}$$

$$occupied : \mathbb{P}(\mathbb{N} \times \mathbb{N})$$

$$\forall x, y : \mathbb{N} \mid (x, y) \in occupied \bullet \\ \quad x < width \land \\ \quad y < height$$

This class has no initial state schema and no operations. It also has no explicit visibility list indicating that all features are visible. The class has a single state variable *occupied* which models the occupied positions of the grid by their x- and y-positions in the grid. The permissible range of these positions is defined by the constants *width* and *height* denoting the width and height of the grid respectively.

A diagrammatic representation of a grid object with $width = 4$, $height = 6$ and $occupied = \{(0,0), (1,2), (2,2), (2,3)\}$ is given in Figure 1.3.

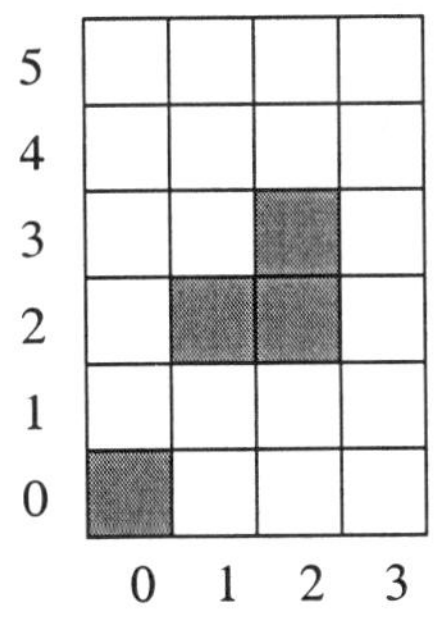

Figure 1.3: Grid object

The playing screen is that portion of the actual computer screen in which blocks can occur. It can be modelled by a grid object whose width is 10 and height is 22. The occupied positions, corresponding to fallen blocks, form a contiguous shape at the bottom of the screen. An example of an instance of the playing screen is shown in Figure 1.4.

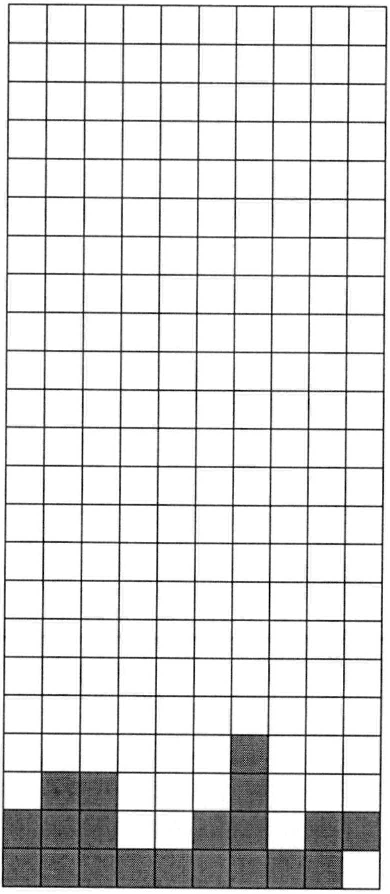

Figure 1.4: Playing screen

The playing screen is, therefore, modelled by a class *Screen* which inherits *Grid* and adds predicates to the state schema equating *width* to 10 and *height* to 22. Rather than specify the condition on the occupied positions also as a predicate of the state schema, we ensure it through the specification of the initial state schema and operations. Initially, at the beginning of a game, the playing screen will have no occupied positions. The class *Screen* has two operations: *AddBlock* corresponding to a block being added to the screen and *RemoveRow* corresponding to a fully occupied row of the screen being removed. The precondition of *AddBlock* ensures that some position occupied by the block is immediately above either the bottom of the playing screen or a previously added block. Unlike in Z, an operation cannot occur outside its precondition: in Z, it can occur but the outcome of the operation is undefined. In Object-Z, an operation is said to be *blocked* — that is, unable to occur — unless its precondition is true. The postcondition of *RemoveRow* ensures that all occupied positions of the playing screen above the removed row are shifted down one position.

Screen

Grid

$$width = 10$$
$$height = 22$$

INIT

$$occupied = \varnothing$$

AddBlock

$$\Delta(occupied)$$
$$occupied? : \mathbb{P}(\mathbb{N} \times \mathbb{N})$$

$$\begin{array}{l} \exists\, x, y : \mathbb{N} \mid (x, y) \in occupied? \bullet \\ \quad (y = 0 \\ \quad \vee \\ \quad (x, y-1) \in occupied) \\ occupied' = occupied \cup occupied? \end{array}$$

RemoveRow

$$\Delta(occupied)$$

$$\begin{array}{l} \exists\, y : 0 \mathinner{..} height - 1 \bullet \\ \quad (\forall\, x : 0 \mathinner{..} width - 1 \bullet (x, y) \in occupied) \wedge \\ \quad occupied' = \{i,j : \mathbb{N} \mid (i,j) \in occupied \wedge j < y\} \\ \qquad\qquad\qquad \cup \\ \qquad\qquad\qquad \{i,j : \mathbb{N} \mid (i,j) \in occupied \wedge j > y \bullet (i, j-1)\} \end{array}$$

The operation *AddBlock* has an input variable *occupied*? denoting the positions of the playing screen occupied by the block. The precondition requires that there exists a position (x, y) occupied by the block which is either at the bottom of the playing screen — $y = 0$ — or immediately above an occupied position — $(x, y-1) \in occupied$. The postcondition requires that the positions occupied by the block are added to the occupied positions of the playing screen.

The precondition of the operation *RemoveRow* requires that there exists a row y in which all positions are occupied — $\forall\, x : 0 \mathinner{..} width - 1 \bullet (x, y) \in occupied$. The postcondition requires that all occupied positions of the playing screen (i,j) below this row — that is, with $j < y$ — remain occupied and all occupied positions (i,j) above the row — that is, with $j > y$ — shift down one row to $(i, j-1)$. The occupied positions in row y are effectively removed from the playing screen.

The blocks in Tetris come in seven different shapes. Each block can be modelled as a square grid object comprising either 4, 9 or 16 positions and with four positions occupied. The different blocks are shown in this form in Figure 1.5.

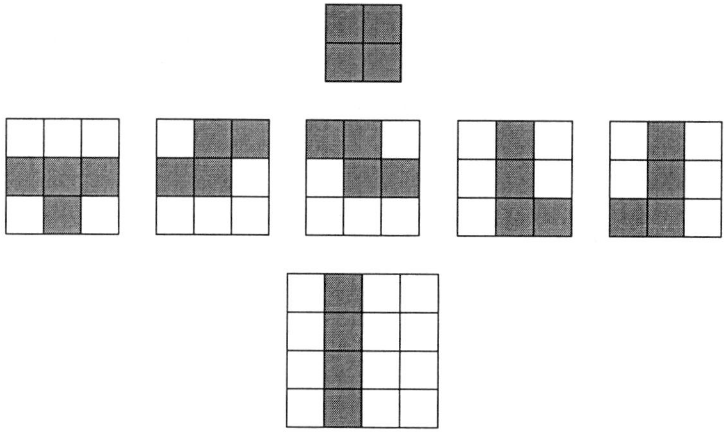

Figure 1.5: Blocks

To specify a general class *Block* from which other block classes can be derived, we again inherit the class *Grid*. Predicates are added to the state schema stating that the width and the height of the grid are equal and that there are four occupied positions. We also add state variables *x_position* and *y_position* denoting the block's position on the playing screen as shown in Figure 1.6.

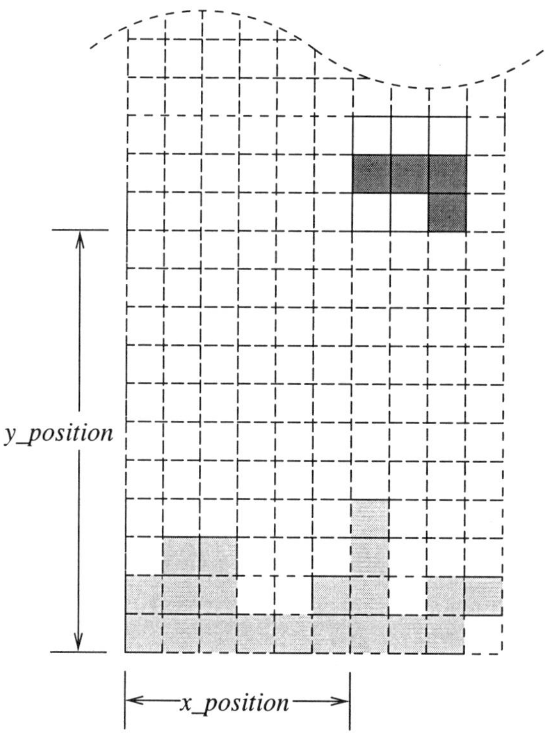

Figure 1.6: Block

$$
\begin{array}{|l}
\hline
\textit{Block} \\
\textit{Grid} \\
\quad
\begin{array}{|l}
\hline
x\_position, y\_position : \mathbb{Z} \\
\hline
width = height \\
\# occupied = 4 \\
\forall x, y : \mathbb{N} \mid (x, y) \in occupied \bullet \\
\qquad 0 \leqslant x\_position + x < 10 \wedge 0 \leqslant y\_position + y \\
\hline
\end{array} \\
\quad
\begin{array}{|l}
\hline
\textit{Init} \\
y\_position = 22 \\
\hline
\end{array} \\
\quad
\begin{array}{|l}
\hline
\textit{MoveRight} \\
\Delta(x\_position) \\
\hline
x\_position' = x\_position + 1 \\
\hline
\end{array} \\
\quad
\begin{array}{|l}
\hline
\textit{MoveLeft} \\
\Delta(x\_position) \\
\hline
x\_position' = x\_position - 1 \\
\hline
\end{array} \\
\quad
\begin{array}{|l}
\hline
\textit{Rotate} \\
\Delta(occupied) \\
\hline
\end{array} \\
\quad
\begin{array}{|l}
\hline
\textit{MoveDown} \\
\Delta(y\_position) \\
\hline
y\_position' = y\_position - 1 \\
\hline
\end{array} \\
\quad
\begin{array}{|l}
\hline
\textit{BeAddedToScreen} \\
occupied! : \mathbb{P}(\mathbb{N} \times \mathbb{N}) \\
\hline
occupied! = \{x, y : \mathbb{N} \mid (x, y) \in occupied \bullet \\
\qquad\qquad (x\_position + x, y\_position + y)\} \\
\hline
\end{array} \\
\hline
\end{array}
$$

The state variables $x\_position$ and $y\_position$ denote the x- and y-positions on the playing screen of the lower left-hand corner of the block. The type of these variables is the set of integers, rather than natural numbers, since the lower left-hand corner of a block can move outside of the playing screen — only the occupied positions of the block must remain within the screen's boundaries.

The predicate of the state schema places the necessary restrictions on the block's movement. The occupied positions of the block offset by $x\_position$ and $y\_position$ must remain within the playing screen — that is, $0 \leqslant x\_position + x < 10$ and $0 \leqslant y\_position + y$. Note that it is not necessary to place an upper limit on $y\_position + y$ because $y\_position$ is initially 22 — so that the block is just above the playing screen

— and no operations of *Block* allow it to move up.

The operations *MoveRight* and *MoveLeft* model the player moving the block one position right or left respectively. This is done by simply incrementing or decrementing the variable $x\_position$. Similarly, the operation *MoveDown* models the computer moving the block down one row by decrementing $y\_position$. These operations will only be enabled when their postconditions satisfy the state schema's predicate. That is, they will only be enabled when, after the operation, the occupied positions of the block remain within the playing screen.

The operation *Rotate* specifies that *occupied* is changed but not how it is changed. This will vary depending on the type of block. The full definition of the operation is deferred, therefore, until *Block* is inherited to specify a particular type of block. Again it is only enabled if, after the operation, the block remains within the playing screen.

The operation *BeAddedToScreen* does not change the state of *Block* — the absence of a Δ-list is equivalent to the empty Δ-list — but simply outputs the screen positions corresponding to the occupied positions of the block. That is, it outputs the occupied positions of the block offset by $x\_position$ and $y\_position$.

The first type of block we specify is the square block shown in Figure 1.7.

Figure 1.7: Square block

It is modelled by a class *Square* which inherits *Block* and adds to the state schema the predicate stating that the width, and therefore the height, of the grid is 2.

```
┌─ Square ──────────────────────────────
│ Block
│
│ ┌──────────────────────────────────
│ │ width = 2
│ └──────────────────────────────────
│
│ ┌─ Rotate ─────────────────────────
│ │ occupied′ = occupied
│ └──────────────────────────────────
└───────────────────────────────────────
```

Since rotating a square block has no effect on the occupied positions — all positions are occupied and remain so — the definition of the *Rotate* operation is completed in this class by adding to it a predicate which states that *occupied* is unchanged. This would necessarily be true even without this predicate, which is added only for clarity, since the inherited state schema includes the predicate $\#occupied = 4$.

The next five types of blocks we specify are polygons. Each can be represented by a grid whose width and height are 3. Hence, we define a general class *Polygon* from which the individual polygon classes can be derived.

Polygon

Block

$$width = 3$$

Rotate

$$\begin{aligned} occupied' = &\{x : \mathbb{N} \mid (0,x) \in occupied \bullet (x,2)\} \\ &\cup \\ &\{x : \mathbb{N} \mid (1,x) \in occupied \bullet (x,1)\} \\ &\cup \\ &\{x : \mathbb{N} \mid (2,x) \in occupied \bullet (x,0)\} \end{aligned}$$

The operation *Rotate*, in this class, is extended with a predicate that moves each occupied grid position to its new position after the block has been rotated in a clockwise direction. Any occupied position $(0,x)$, where x is a number from 0 to 2, is moved to $(x,2)$. Similarly, any occupied position $(1,x)$ or $(2,x)$ is moved to $(x,1)$ or $(x,0)$ respectively. For example, the position $(1,0)$ will be moved to $(0,1)$ and the position $(0,2)$ to $(2,2)$. This is represented diagrammatically in Figure 1.8.

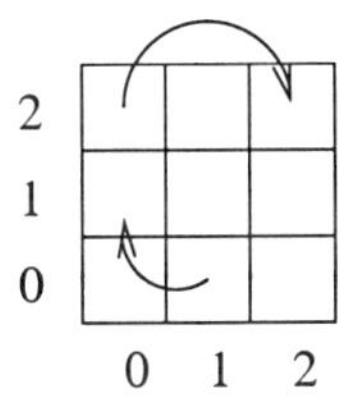

Figure 1.8: Polygon rotation

The class *Polygon* models more types of blocks than the five we wish to specify. To specify the individual blocks, we define subclasses of *Polygon* which have a particular initial configuration of occupied positions. For example, consider the T block, named after its resemblance to the letter "T", shown in Figure 1.9.

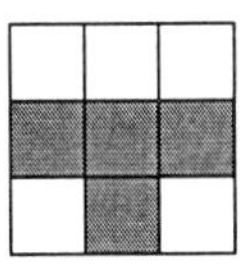

Figure 1.9 T block

This block is specified by the class T as a *Polygon* whose initial set of occupied positions is $\{(0,1),(1,0),(1,1),(2,1)\}$.

T

Polygon

INIT

$$occupied = \{(0,1),(1,0),(1,1),(2,1)\}$$

The other four blocks — the S, Z, L and reverse-L blocks — are shown in Figure 1.10.

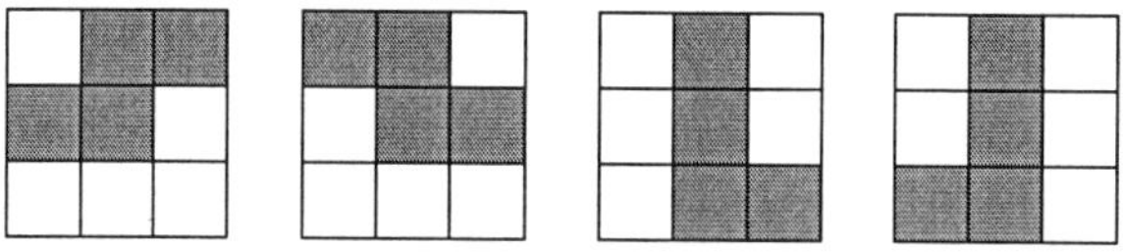

Figure 1.10: S, Z, L and reverse-L blocks

They are specified in a similar fashion by the classes S, Z, L and $ReverseL$ below.

S

$Polygon$

INIT

$occupied = \{(0,1),(1,1),(1,2),(2,2)\}$

Z

$Polygon$

INIT

$occupied = \{(0,2),(1,1),(1,2),(2,1)\}$

L

$Polygon$

INIT

$occupied = \{(1,0),(1,1),(1,2),(2,0)\}$

$ReverseL$

$Polygon$

INIT

$occupied = \{(0,0),(1,0),(1,1),(1,2)\}$

The final type of block to be specified is the rectangle block. This block has two possible positions — vertical and horizontal — as shown in Figure 1.11.

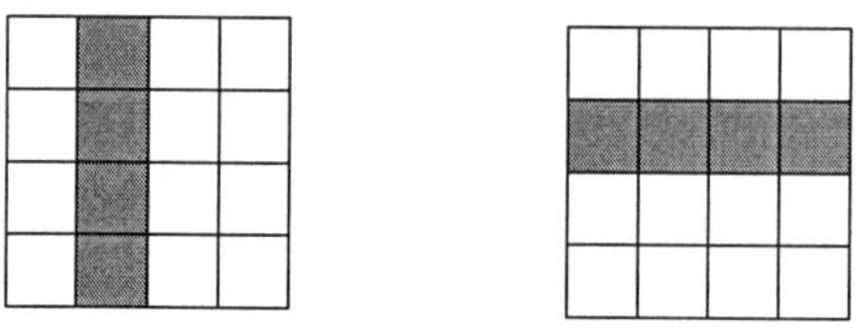

Figure 1.11: Rectangle block

It is modelled by a class *Rectangle* which inherits *Block* and adds to the state schema a predicate stating that the width (and height) of the grid is 4, and a predicate stating that the rectangle is in one of the two positions — vertical or horizontal — shown in Figure 1.11.

Rectangle

Block

$$width = 4$$
$$(occupied = \{(1,0),(1,1),(1,2),(1,3)\}$$
$$\vee$$
$$occupied = \{(0,2),(1,2),(2,2),(3,2)\})$$

INIT

$$occupied = \{(1,0),(1,1),(1,2),(1,3)\}$$

Rotate

$$occupied' \neq occupied$$

The class *Rectangle* makes the assumption that the rectangle block is in the vertical position initially. The *Rotate* operation simply switches the position of the block from vertical to horizontal or horizontal to vertical.

The inheritance hierarchy of the specification is presented in Figure 1.12.

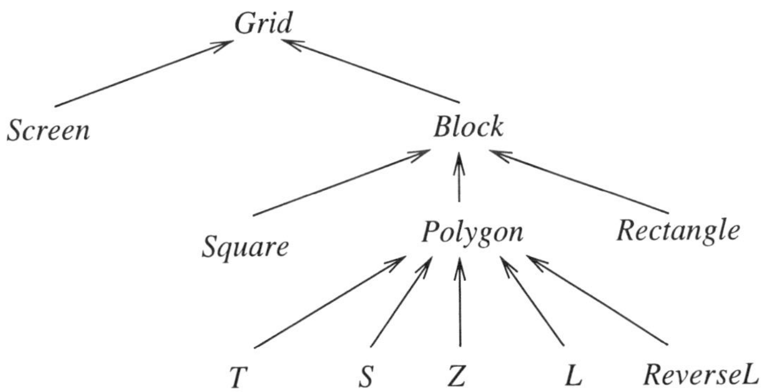

Figure 1.12: Grid hierarchy

The class of the object representing the falling block in the game of Tetris will be one of those modelling a type of block — *Square*, *T*, *S*, *Z*, *L*, *ReverseL* or *Rectangle*. We will therefore require the following polymorphic declaration.

$block : \downarrow Block$

To ensure the actual class of *block* is not *Block* or *Polygon*, however, we will also require the following predicate.

$block \notin Block \wedge block \notin Polygon$

The game of Tetris is specified by a class *Tetris* whose interface includes six operations. Three of these — *MoveRight*, *MoveLeft* and *Rotate* — model the player's options of moving the falling block left or right or rotating it respectively. The other three operations — *MoveDown*, *AddBlock* and *RemoveRow* — modelling a block moving down one row, a block being added to the screen, and a row being removed, are controlled by the computer.

Tetris

$$\upharpoonright(screen, block, score, \mathrm{INIT}, MoveRight, MoveLeft, Rotate, MoveDown, AddBlock, RemoveRow)$$

$$screen : Screen$$
$$block : \downarrow Block$$
$$score : \mathbb{N}$$

$$block \notin Block \land block \notin Polygon$$
$$\forall x, y : \mathbb{N} \mid (x, y) \in block.occupied \bullet (block.x\_position + x, block.y\_position + y) \notin screen.occupied$$

INIT

$$screen.\mathrm{INIT}$$
$$block.\mathrm{INIT}$$
$$score = 0$$

$$MoveRight \mathrel{\widehat{=}} block.MoveRight$$
$$MoveLeft \mathrel{\widehat{=}} block.MoveLeft$$
$$Rotate \mathrel{\widehat{=}} block.Rotate$$
$$MoveDown \mathrel{\widehat{=}} block.MoveDown$$

NewBlock

$$\Delta(block)$$

$$block'.\mathrm{INIT}$$

$$AddBlock \mathrel{\widehat{=}} (block.BeAddedToScreen \parallel screen.AddBlock) \land NewBlock$$

AdvanceScore

$$\Delta(score)$$

$$score' = score + 10$$

$$RemoveRow \mathrel{\widehat{=}} screen.RemoveRow \land AdvanceScore$$

The class has three variables — *screen* and *block* denoting the identities of the objects representing the playing screen and falling block respectively, and *score* denoting the player's score. The predicates of the state schema ensure that *block* identifies an object whose class is one of the seven types of blocks of the game, and that the block does not overlap with occupied positions of the screen. The latter predicate restricts the operations which change the block's position or orientation — *MoveRight*, *MoveLeft*, *Rotate* and *MoveDown*.

Initially, at the beginning of a game of Tetris, both the screen and block objects identified by *screen* and *block* are in their initial states. The screen has no occupied positions, the block's occupied positions are configured according to its class — that is, to the type of block it is — and the block is positioned just above the playing screen. The player's score is initially zero.

The operations *MoveRight*, *MoveLeft*, *Rotate* and *MoveDown* model the block object undergoing operations *MoveRight*, *MoveLeft*, *Rotate* and *MoveDown* of its class respectively.

The operation *NewBlock* changes the variable *block* so that it identifies a new block object. The predicate of the operation requires that this new block object is in its initial state. *NewBlock* is not in the class's visibility list but is used in the definition of the operation *AddBlock*. It is conjoined with a parallel composition of the block object outputting its occupied positions, offset by its position on the screen, and the screen object adding them to its occupied positions. The output variable *occupied*! of *block.BeAddedToScreen* is equated with the input variable *occupied*? of *screen.Addblock* to achieve the necessary communication.

The operation *AdvanceScore* advances the player's score by 10 points. It is also not in the class's visibility list but is conjoined with the operation expression *screen.RemoveRow* to form the operation *RemoveRow*.

The Tetris case study has illustrated the use of the major object-oriented constructs of Object-Z. *Classes* were used to model the playing screen and blocks of the game. *Inheritance* enabled these classes to be incrementally constructed from a common grid class. *Objects* of the screen and block classes were used to specify the Tetris game. *Polymorphism* was exploited to model the falling block as one of a number of different types of blocks.

The remainder of this book provides a complete description of the Object-Z language. It will enable you to confidently construct similar Object-Z specifications and also specifications of much greater complexity. It is intended as a reference manual to keep by your side as you use and learn to use Object-Z.

2

Semantic Basis

Object-Z not only extends the syntax of Z but also the semantic universe in which specifications are given meaning. In order to write correct Object-Z specifications and fully utilize Object-Z's expressive power, it is essential for the specifier to have an understanding of the basis of this semantic universe. In particular, it is necessary for the specifier to have a sound understanding of Object-Z's notion of *object identity* and its effects on modularity and compositionality.

Support for object identity in Object-Z presents a major departure from the semantics of Z. It allows variables to be declared which, rather than directly representing a value, refer to a value in much the same way as pointers in a programming language. A semantics supporting such variables is called a *reference semantics*.

The reference semantics of Object-Z impacts on the use of the language in two main ways. Firstly, it facilitates the refinement of Object-Z specifications to code in an object-oriented programming language. Object-oriented programming languages also have reference semantics and so similar system structuring can be used in both the specification and implementation.

Secondly, the use of reference semantics profoundly influences system design. When an object is merely referenced by another, it is not encapsulated in any way by the referencing object. Hence, changes to a referenced object generally have no effect on the state of the referencing object — objects are independent entities and systems are structured as collections of such entities. Furthermore, more than one variable can reference a given object allowing an object to play more than one role. In addition, in Object-Z's reference semantics, objects of a given class can be referred to in a specification before that class is defined. This enables the specification of systems in which self and mutual recursion are possible.

In this chapter, we provide an informal outline of the reference semantics of Object-Z. It is not the intent of the chapter to present a mathematical model of the Object-Z language but to explain the concepts on which such a mathematical model can be built. The chapter has two main goals. Firstly, it details the differences between standard types and values in Z and those introduced into Object-Z to support object identity and the notion of systems as collections of independent entities. Secondly, it highlights the consequences of adopting a reference semantics. In particular, the effects on system modularity and compositionality are examined in the light of *object coupling* — that is, inter-object dependencies — and *object aliasing* — that is, multiple references to the same object.

2.1 Object Identity

Object identity refers to that property of an object which enables it to be distinguished from all other objects. Generally, objects can be distinguished by their class or, if they belong to the same class, by the values of their attributes — that is, constants and state variables. However, to distinguish objects of the same class and with the same attribute values, object identity is required.

Object identity also models the notion that objects are *persistent* entities which continue to exist in a uniquely identifiable way despite changes to their state. That is, the identity of an object can be continuously used to refer to that object as its state is changed by the application of operations. With a reference semantics such as that of Object-Z, object identity also ensures that objects persist even when the variables that refer to them change.

2.1.1 Types and values

Object identity is modelled in Object-Z by associating with each class a set of values. The sets for different classes are disjoint. For any class, other than one which has no objects (see Section 2.2), this set is countably infinite. Each value associated with a class identifies a distinct object of the class. That is, the values identify distinct objects whose behaviours conform to the definitions within the class. The values themselves, however, are independent of the definitions within the class.

An object identity is declared by using a class as a type. For example given a class A, the declaration $a : A$ defines a variable a whose value is the identity of an object of class A. When class A has no objects, the declaration is not satisfiable and, hence, introduces into the construct in which it occurs — which may be an axiomatic definition or a schema for example — the predicate false. In the remainder of this section, we ignore such classes. Their presence in specifications is discussed at the beginning of Section 2.2.

In the case of classes with generic parameters, the declaration of an identity requires the parameters to be instantiated. For example, given the class $C[X, Y]$ where X and Y are generic parameters, $c : C[\mathbb{N}, \mathbb{B}]$ declares c as the identity of an object whose behaviour is consistent with that defined by $C[X, Y]$ when X is instantiated with the set of natural numbers and Y with the set of Boolean values. Note that the parameters may be instantiated either with types — as in this example — or with the generic parameters of the context — for example, the system class — in which the object is declared.

An object identity can also be declared polymorphically — that is, so that it can be assigned the identity of an object from one of a collection of classes. For example, given an inheritance hierarchy where each subclass has at least the visible features of the class A at the top of the hierarchy, $a : \downarrow A$ declares an identity a of an object of class A or one of its subclasses. Note that the subclasses to which a can belong include those defined both before and after the declaration $a : \downarrow A$ — that is, all subclasses of A in the specification.

Object-Z also has another, more flexible, notion of polymorphism called *class union*. Class union allows the declaration of an identity of an object of one of an arbitrary set of classes. For example, given classes A and B, the declaration $a : A \cup B$ declares an identity a of an object of either class A or B.

The types associated with classes and those constructed from these using class union are the only additional types in Object-Z. Types of the form $\downarrow A$ are just a special case of class union. These additional types correspond to sets of object identities which makes them notably different to standard Z types.

In Z, types are either basic types — such as the set of integers $\mathbb{Z}$ — or constructed from basic types. The kinds of constructed types are set types, Cartesian product types and schema types. All entities in a specification are given a type and their values are, therefore, basic values — such as -1, 0 or 15 — or constructed from basic values and the values of other entities within the specification. This leads to specifications in which the entire system is a single entity whose value is composed of the values of other entities. For example, consider the schema S.

S

$a : A$
$b : B$

This schema has two variables — a of type A and b of type B. If A and B are standard Z types then an instance s of the schema S can be represented diagrammatically as in Figure 2.1. Boxes in this diagram represent values in the semantic domain. The name above a box represents the variable which has that value and the name in the top left-hand corner of the box represents the variable's type.

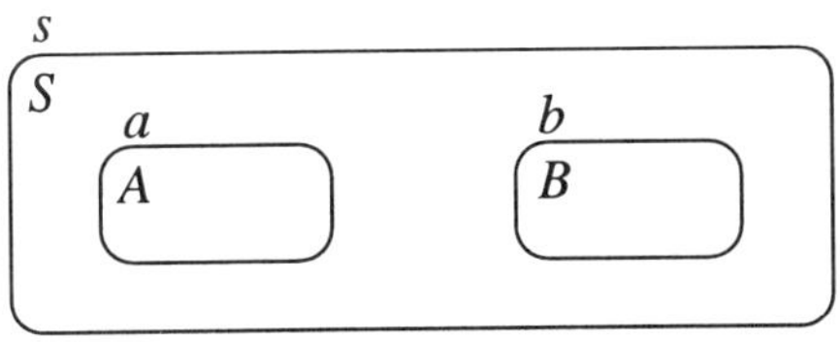

Figure 2.1: Representation of standard Z values

The diagram emphasizes the fact that variables a and b are part of the schema instance s. Any changes to either of these variables changes s as well.

Object identities differ from standard Z values in that they are used to reference a value in the semantic domain rather than represent it directly. This leads to a different way of structuring specifications.

If the types A and B of the schema S were class types then an instance s of schema S could be represented diagrammatically as in Figure 2.2. The semantic value of an object identity is represented by an arrow pointing from the variable to which the identity is assigned to the object which it references.

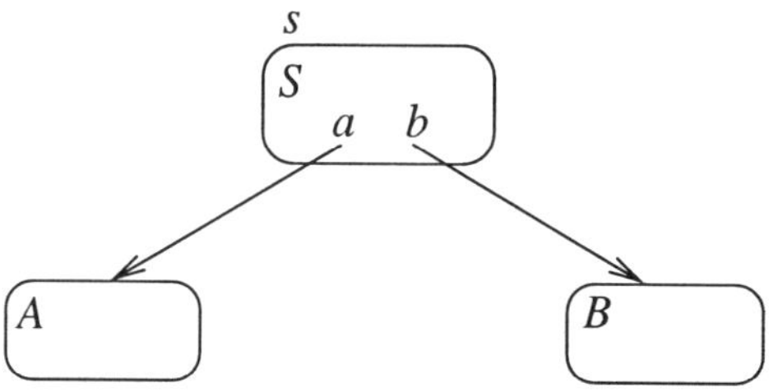

Figure 2.2: Representation of object identities

The diagram, in this case, emphasizes the fact that the schema instance s is independent of the objects referenced by a and b. The value of these objects are, in fact, not directly represented by any variable of the specification. Their existence, however, is indicated by the variables a and b whose values are their identities. The reference semantics allows systems to be constructed, in this way, as collections of independent entities. An instance of the system specification, which could be a schema but is more commonly a class, references either directly or indirectly, via its referenced objects, all of the objects which constitute the system. This is in contrast to the traditional structuring of systems in Z as single entities.

2.1.2 Forward declaration

Another difference with standard Z semantics arises from the fact that object identities may be declared in a specification before the class of the referenced object is defined. For example, a variable declaration $a : A$ may occur prior to the definition of class A. This is possible since the set of object identities associated with the class A is independent of the actual definition of the class A. We refer to $a : A$ as a *forward declaration* of a variable of A.

This feature provides greater flexibility when specifying systems than would otherwise be possible. For example, an object may refer to an object of the same class. To illustrate this, consider a system for recording information about people, including who their father is. The specification of this system may use the class $Person$ below. (Details irrelevant to the example have been elided from the class.)

Person

$father : Person$

$\ldots$

$\ldots$

The class $Person$ is used as a type in the declaration of the state variable $father$ — that is, before the class $Person$ has been fully defined. This structuring is particularly useful for modelling recursive data types such as lists and trees. As with these data types, some "null" value of the class $Person$ would be required, in this example, so that a finite system of records could be defined.

As a more obvious example of the use of a class type before the class definition, consider specifying a subclass *Father* of *Person* to model information about people who are fathers. The record system could then use the following classes.

```
┌─ Person ───────────────────────────
│ ┌──────────────────────────────────
│ │ father : Father
│ │ ...
│ └──────────────────────────────────
│ ...
└────────────────────────────────────
```

```
┌─ Father ───────────────────────────
│ Person
│ ...
└────────────────────────────────────
```

When a class is inherited by another, its definitions are included in the other and combined with them where appropriate. Therefore, the definition of a superclass, such as *Person* above, must always precede any subclass, such as *Father*. Hence, the declaration $father : Father$, in this example, must precede the definition of *Father*.

As a final example, suppose the record system is for a school. Rather than a class *Person* this system has a class *Student* and another class *Father* for modelling the fathers of students.

```
┌─ Student ──────────────────────────
│ ┌──────────────────────────────────
│ │ father : Father
│ │ ...
│ └──────────────────────────────────
│ ...
└────────────────────────────────────
```

```
┌─ Father ───────────────────────────
│ ┌──────────────────────────────────
│ │ students : ℙ Student
│ │ ...
│ └──────────────────────────────────
│ ...
└────────────────────────────────────
```

In this case, there is no inheritance relation between the classes and they could occur in any order. However, because the referencing is mutual — that is, *Student* references an object of *Father* and *Father* references objects of *Student* — once again this is only possible using a forward declaration. Note that the structuring in this case is only possible with a reference semantics. It would not be possible to have the value of a father entity as part of the value of a student entity and, at the same time, the value of the student entity as part of the value of the father entity.

2.1.3 Self-reference

Another type of structuring that is only possible with a reference semantics is that in which an object references itself. Consider, for example, a system which records information about employees including who their boss is. The specification of this system may use the class *Employee* below.

```
Employee
  | boss : Employee
  | ...
  ...
```

The type of the variable *boss* is *Employee* to reflect the fact that a boss is also an employee. Since this variable can identify any object of class *Employee* it is possible that an employee is his or her own boss — that is, he or she is self-employed. Self-referencing can be explicitly specified in Object-Z using a reserved word *self*. This word can be used within a class definition and denotes the object identity of an object of the class. For example, a self-employed employee could be specified by the class *SelfEmployed* below.

```
SelfEmployed
  Employee
  | boss = self
```

The *Person* class in the first example and the *Father* class in the second would have similarly required a state predicate $father \neq self$. It is important for the specifier to be aware of the possibility of self-reference in a specification and include such predicates where required.

2.2 Objects

The state of an object assigns values to the attributes — state variables and constants — of its class which not only satisfy the class's state predicate and any predicates associated with the constant definitions, but also correspond to the values of a state which is reachable from the class's initial state via the application of its operations. A class which has an unsatisfiable initial condition — either because the initial state schema's predicate evaluates to false, or the class has no initial state schema and its state schema's predicate or a predicate associated with a constant definition evaluates to false — has no objects. All other classes have a countably infinite set of objects — one for each object identity associated with the class type.

Object-Z does not support the creation and destruction of objects. Each object which can be referenced by a specification exists throughout the evolution of the specified system — even in the case when it is never actually referenced. While this would not be feasible in a programming language where issues of memory usage and efficiency are important, it is not a problem in the abstract world of a specification.

2.2.1 Objects vs. object identities

The distinction between variables which denote object identities and the identified objects themselves is central to Object-Z. While the former can be accessed and changed directly by the specifier, the latter cannot. For example, consider the following class B where A is another class in the specification.

B

$a : A$

Op
$\Delta(a)$

$a' \neq a$

The operation Op of this class directly changes the object identity referred to by the state variable a. Before the operation, a refers to a particular object of class A and after the operation it refers to a different object of class A. Both of these objects are unaffected by the operation.

In contrast, the only way an object can be changed is via the application of one of its class's operations using the dot notation. The use of this notation is restricted to respect the class's interface. That is, an object can only be changed by visible operations of its class. Similarly, information about the state of an object — the value of an attribute or whether the object is in an initial state — can only be accessed via the dot notation and only when the information is visible.

Accessing attributes

Selected attributes of a class are made visible by their inclusion in the class's visibility list. Given an object of the class, such visible attributes may be accessed via the dot notation . For example, if class A has a visible attribute x, given the declaration $a : A$, $a.x$ denotes the value of the variable x in the state of the object referenced by a.

It is not possible to access the attributes of referenced objects in the post-states of operations. The notation $a'.x$ denotes, not the post-state value of the variable x of the object referenced by a, but the pre-state value of the variable x of the object referenced by a'. If $a' = a$ (for example, when a is the primary variable of a class and not included in the operation's Δ-list) then $a'.x = a.x$ even when the x value of the object identified by a is changed. Hence, it is not possible to explicitly define a change to a referenced object's state in terms of its attributes.

Checking initial conditions

The initial state schema of a class comprises a predicate stating the conditions of being in an initial state in terms of the class's attributes. When *INIT* is in the class's visibility list, this predicate may be accessed via the dot notation to check whether or not an object of the class is in an initial state. For example, if $a : A$ where A is a class with *INIT* visible, then $a.\mathit{INIT}$ denotes a predicate which is true whenever the state of a satisfies the initial state predicate of A.

Although a predicate such as $a.\mathit{INIT}$ is usually used to identify an object which is in an initial state because it has not yet undergone any operations, it also evaluates to true for an object which has undergone operations but returned to an initial state — that is, returned to a state which satisfies the predicate of its class's initial state schema. In any Object-Z specification, using such an object is identical to using an object which has not undergone any operations.

Applying operations

An operation definition in a class may include a Δ-list which lists which primary variables of the class may change — secondary variables may be changed by any operation — declarations of auxiliary variables such as input and output variables and predicates defining the operation's pre- and postconditions. A visible operation is applied to an object using the dot notation. For example, given $a : A$ where A is a class with a visible operation Op, $a.Op$ denotes an operation which models the application of Op to a.

The operation $a.Op$ does not change any variables of the class in which it is defined. Although the state of the object referenced by a is changed by $a.Op$, the identity a itself is not. Therefore, the Δ-list of $a.Op$ is empty. The auxiliary variables of $a.Op$ are the same as those of Op and are declared implicitly. The pre- and postconditions reflect those of Op. The operation $a.Op$ is applicable whenever the state of a satisfies the precondition of Op and changes the state of a to satisfy the postcondition of Op.

The operation $a.Op$ cannot be used in the predicate part of another operation. It may, however, be combined with other operations using the operation operators of Object-Z detailed in Section 3.7.3.

2.2.2 Forward declaration revisited

When a forward declaration of an object identity is made in Object-Z, it is possible to access the visible features of the identified object using the dot notation. This allows the specification of systems in a top-down fashion. The class specifying a system in terms of its component objects and their interactions can appear before the classes specifying the components. This can increase the clarity of a specification by providing the context in which the components occur as motivation for their definitions. It can also provide a more intuitive development path for the specifier.

Accessing the visible features associated with forwardly declared object identities is also useful in recursive specifications. In particular, it is useful for specifying recursive data structures. For example, consider specifying a sorted binary tree where each node has a value of type natural number and a left and right subtree. Each value in the left subtree is less than that in the node and each value in the right subtree is greater than or equal to that in the node. The sorted binary tree is specified by the class *Tree*.

$$
\begin{array}{l}
\textit{Tree} \\
\hline
\quad null : \mathbb{B} \\
\quad val : \mathbb{N} \\
\quad left\_tree, right\_tree : \textit{Tree} \\
\quad \Delta \\
\quad nodes : \mathbb{P}\,\textit{Tree} \\
\hline
\quad \langle left\_tree.nodes, \{self\}, right\_tree.nodes \rangle \text{ partitions } nodes \\
\quad \forall\, t : left\_tree.nodes \bullet t.null \lor t.val < val \\
\quad \forall\, t : right\_tree.nodes \bullet t.null \lor t.val \geqslant val \\
\hline
\textsc{Init} \\
\hline
\quad null \land left\_tree.\textsc{Init} \land right\_tree.\textsc{Init} \\
\hline
\textit{Insert} \mathrel{\widehat=} [\Delta(null, val)\;\; v? : \mathbb{N} \mid null \land val' = v? \land \neg\, null'] \\
\qquad\qquad [\!] \\
\qquad\qquad [\neg\, null] \land (left\_tree.\textit{Insert}\ [\!]\ right\_tree.\textit{Insert})
\end{array}
$$

This class specifies the functionality of the sorted binary tree abstractly by defining an infinite tree structure into which values can be inserted. This allows us to avoid the details of the construction of the tree. Although we would need to include these details when refining this specification to an implementation, it is simpler to ignore them at this higher level of abstraction. To distinguish the inserted values from those initially in the tree structure a Boolean-valued variable *null* is used. When *null* is true the actual tree (or subtree) is empty — that is, no values have been inserted.

Apart from *null*, the state of the tree is modelled by three primary variables — *val* denoting the value of the root node of the tree, and *left_tree* and *right_tree* denoting the root node's left and right subtrees respectively. The class also has a secondary variable *nodes* denoting the set of all nodes in the tree represented by the subtrees of which they are the root.

The first predicate of the state schema defines *nodes* recursively in terms of the variable *nodes* of *left_tree* and *right_tree*. The set *nodes* is partitioned by these sets and the set containing the root node represented by *self*. The partitioning ensures that the three sets are disjoint as required for a tree. The properties of the tree are then specified in terms of *nodes* in the second and third predicates of the state schema.

Initially, a tree is empty. This implies that all subtrees of the tree are empty. Hence, as well as *null* being true for the root node, it must be true for all nodes of the tree. This is specified recursively in the initial condition by stating that the left and right subtrees are also in their initial states.

The operation *Insert* is also defined recursively as follows. If the tree is empty — that is, *null* is true — the value of the tree's root node is assigned to the input value $v?$ and $null$ becomes false indicating that the tree is no longer empty. If, on the other hand, the tree is not empty, the $Insert$ operation is applied to either $left\_tree$ or $right\_tree$. Only one of the operations $left\_tree.Insert$ and $right\_tree.Insert$ will be able to occur since the state schema's predicate must be true after the operation. That is, if the input value is less than the root node's value then only $left\_tree.Insert$ will be able to occur and if it is greater than or equal to the root node's value then only $right\_tree.Insert$ will be able to occur.

Such recursive operation definitions can be expressed in a non-recursive form using fixed-point theory. For example, the selection of the node to which the value $v?$ is inserted in $Insert$ could have been specified as a choice over all the nodes in the tree such that the chosen node was empty, all nodes between the root node and the chosen node were not empty, and the invariant (that the tree is sorted) is maintained. A general technique for deriving non-recursive definitions of recursive operations is presented in Section 3.7.5.

2.3 Modularity and Compositionality

A modular specification is one which comprises a number of separate parts, or modules, each of which can be understood in isolation. For example, an object-oriented specification is modular due to the structure provided by its classes. Related to modularity is the notion of compositionality. A compositional specification is one which is modular and where the meaning of the overall specification can be determined from the meaning of its modules.

Compositionality enables the processes of refining and reasoning about specifications to be simplified. A compositional specification can be refined by refining one or more of its modules in isolation – that is, without reference to the rest of the specification. Similarly, properties of such a specification may be derived from the properties of the modules derived in isolation. Due to its reference semantics, however, not all specifications in Object-Z are compositional.

2.3.1 Object coupling

Since a class may refer to the attributes of an object it references, it may place constraints on that object's state. When these constraints occur as part of the state predicate, they must be maintained by each operation of the class. This can cause the possible states an object can be in to be restricted, or a relationship between the attributes of one object and those of another to be maintained. Such dependencies between objects are referred to as *object coupling*.

Object coupling can be used to simplify specifications. Values derived from the values of the attributes of one or more objects can be represented by a state variable and, hence, accessed directly. This affects the behaviour of the objects, however, and, in many cases, the compositionality of the specification. As an example, consider the following class B where A is a class with a state variable $x : \mathbb{N}$.

$$\begin{array}{|l}
\underline{B\qquad\qquad\qquad\qquad\qquad\qquad\qquad\qquad} \\
\quad \begin{array}{|l}
a : A \\
y : \mathbb{N} \\
\hline
a.x = y
\end{array} \\
\\
\quad \underline{IncrementY\qquad\qquad\qquad} \\
\quad \begin{array}{|l}
\Delta(y) \\
\hline
y' = y + 1
\end{array} \\
\hline
\end{array}$$

If the operation $IncrementY$ occurs, y is incremented and, so that the state predicate holds in the operation's post-state, $a.x$ would need to be incremented as well. Whether the operation can occur for an object identified by $b : B$, however, depends on the operations of A and the specification in which b is declared.

The operation $b.IncrementY$ cannot change the object identified by $b.a$ – this can only be done by the application of an operation to $b.a$. It requires, however, that the object does change and this is only possible if an operation which changes it in the desired way occurs concurrently with $b.IncrementY$. For example, if A has an operation $IncrementX$ which increments the variable x then $b.IncrementY$ can occur in the following specified system.

$$\begin{array}{|l}
\underline{C\qquad\qquad\qquad\qquad\qquad\qquad\qquad\qquad} \\
\quad \begin{array}{|l}
a : A \\
b : B \\
\hline
b.a = a
\end{array} \\
\\
IncrementXY \mathrel{\widehat=} a.IncrementX \land b.IncrementY \\
\hline
\end{array}$$

The state predicate of class B restricts not only the behaviour of any object identified by $b : B$ but also the object identified by $b.a$. This object cannot undergo any operation which changes its attribute x unless an operation which similarly changes $b.y$ occurs concurrently. This dependency does not allow a specification including the class B to be refined in a compositional manner.

For example, consider the case when A, rather than having an operation to increment x, has an operation $IncreaseX$ to increase x by any amount. On application of the operation, the amount by which x increases is chosen nondeterministically. If this operation were applied to the object identified by $b.a$ concurrently with the application of $IncrementY$ to the object identified by b then the amount by which x is increased would effectively be constrained to 1. Therefore, any refinement of A which reduced the nondeterminism of $IncreaseX$ so that x could no longer be increased by 1, would not lead to a refinement of the overall system.

Appropriate proof obligations related to object coupling need to be discharged, therefore, before a specification is refined in a compositional manner. The exact nature of these proof obligations and that of compositional refinement in Object-Z are not discussed in this book.

2.3.2 Object aliasing

Object aliasing occurs whenever two or more variables in a specification refer to the same object. These variables may be declared in a single class to identify different roles of the object. For example, a person object may reference another person object as both its "mother" and "next of kin". The variables may also be declared in different classes to model the object being shared between subsystems of the specified system. For example, a memory component may be shared between several processors in a multiprocessor system.

Although aliasing is useful for specifying such systems, it can also limit what can be deduced about specified systems in a compositional manner. Often a system comprises one or more subsystems — modelled by component objects which reference other objects. The objects of a subsystem can also be referenced by objects external to the subsystem — other subsystems or the system object itself. Such external referencing can be used to effect changes on the objects other than those changes specified by the subsystem's operations. For example, consider the following class A where C is a class with a visible operation Op.

```
┌─ A ─────────────────────────────
│ ┌───────────────────────────
│ │ a, b : C
│ ├──────────
│ │ a ≠ b
│ └───────────────────────────
│ OpA ≙ a.Op
└─────────────────────────────────
```

The class A models a system comprising two distinct objects of class C referenced by the state variables a and b. The operation OpA changes the object referenced by a according to the operation Op of C. Although the object referenced by b is not mentioned in the definition of this operation, if there is a possibility of external referencing, we cannot deduce that it remains unchanged when OpA occurs. For example, consider the case where an object of class A is a subsystem of the system specified by the following class B.

```
┌─ B ─────────────────────────────
│ ┌───────────────────────────
│ │ a : A
│ │ c : C
│ └───────────────────────────
│ OpB ≙ a.OpA ∧ c.Op
└─────────────────────────────────
```

The class has two state variables a and c referencing objects of classes A and C respectively. When OpB occurs, the object referenced by a undergoes the operation OpA and that referenced by c undergoes the operation Op. If $a.b$ and c reference the same object — that is, $a.b$ and c are aliases — then, when OpB occurs, the object referenced by a undergoes OpA and that referenced by $a.b$ undergoes the operation Op. Hence, when reasoning about OpA of class A, the most we can deduce about the object referenced by b is that if it does change then it changes according to an operation of class C.

This limitation on what can be deduced about the subsystems of a system applies also to the system itself. No formal distinction is made between those classes which define subsystems and that which defines the entire system. However, often there is an informal understanding that there are no further external object references. That is, we have specified a closed system. In such cases, we may assume that any object not changed by a particular operation remains unchanged.

2.3.3 Object containment

Often we wish to restrict the possibility of external referencing. For example, consider a bank which references a set of customer objects and a set of account objects. The bank is specified by the class *Bank* where *Customer* and *Account* are classes defined elsewhere in the specification.

Bank

$$customers : \mathbb{P}\, Customer$$
$$accounts : \mathbb{P}\, Account$$

...

To specify a banking system comprising a set of banks, we need to restrict the external referencing to each of the bank subsystems. Although a customer can be a customer at a number of banks, the accounts at different banks are distinct. Such a system is specified by the class *BankingSytsem*.

BankingSystem

$$banks : \mathbb{P}\, Bank$$

$$\forall\, b_1, b_2 : banks \mid b_1 \neq b_2 \bullet b_1.accounts \cap b_2.accounts = \varnothing$$

...

The state predicate restricts referencing between the bank subsystems. That is, while a customer object may be referenced by a number of bank objects, an account object may only be referenced by one bank object. The conceptual difference between customers and accounts is that the customers of a bank interact with the bank whereas the accounts are part of the bank. Therefore, we say that the account objects are *contained* in the bank subsystem.

This notion of object containment can be captured by predicates such as that in *BankingSystem*. However, such predicates become unwieldy in large specifications. Furthermore, the constraint is really one on banks and not banking systems. That is, the notion that a bank contains its accounts should be specified as part of the *Bank* class. To facilitate this, Object-Z has a specific notation to model object containment. This notation enables the specifier to state that objects are contained in a system when they are declared. For example, consider the system defined by the schema S below.

S

$a : C_{©}$
$b : C$

The system comprises two objects of class C referenced by the variables a and b. The object referenced by a is contained in the system as denoted by the subscript © appended to the class name. An instance s of the schema is represented diagrammatically in Figure 2.3. The contained object is represented by a referenced, and hence independent entity, which is within the box defining the schema instance.

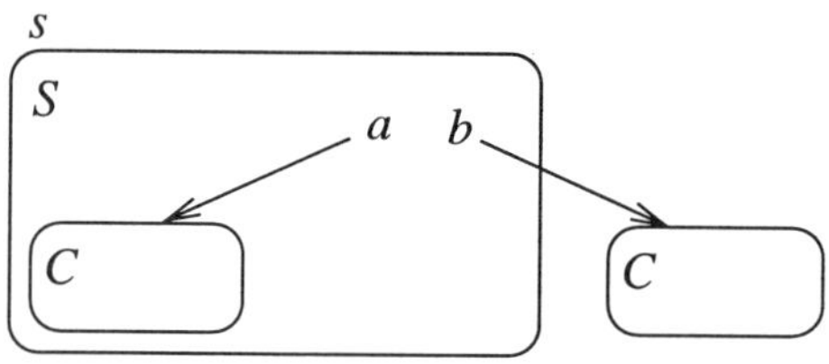

Figure 2.3: Representation of object containment

The diagram emphasizes the fact that an object can only be directly contained by one system. When an object a is contained by a system s and s is contained by a larger system t, then t is said to indirectly contain a.

The bank could be respecified using the containment notation as follows.

Bank

$customers : \mathbb{P}\, Customer$
$accounts : \mathbb{P}\, Account_{©}$

$\ldots$

Since the account objects of a bank system are contained, no two banks can reference the same account. The banking system is hence respecified simply as follows.

$$
\begin{array}{|l}
\textit{BankingSystem} \\
\hline
\begin{array}{|l}
banks : \mathbb{P}\, Bank \\
\hline
\end{array} \\
\ldots \\
\hline
\end{array}
$$

Although, in this example, there is no aliasing of account objects, it should be noted that object containment does not, in general, prevent aliasing. Contained objects may be referenced by many objects in a specified system. However, they can only be directly contained by one object. Hence, when all referenced objects of a certain class are contained, as in the example, aliasing between these objects cannot occur.

3

Syntactic Constructs

An Object-Z specification, like a Z specification, comprises a list of formal paragraphs — type definitions, axiomatic definitions, global predicates, schema definitions and class definitions — interleaved with informal explanatory text and diagrams. As in Z, line breaks in axiomatic definitions and schema definitions, including those that occur within class definitions, are interpreted as semicolons — that is, as declaration or predicate separators — except when such an interpretation is syntactically invalid, in which case they are, as in other parts of the specification, ignored.

There are, however, two notable differences between the form of a Z specification and one in Object-Z. The first is the strict ordering and roles of schemas within a class definition. In Z, whether the initial state schema appears before or after the operation schemas of a specification, for example, is, in most cases, irrelevant. Also, the role of a schema is based on informal conventions. These conventions can change between specifications. For example, the initial state schema of a specification is usually defined by extending the state schema with additional predicates defining the initial condition. However, some Z users prefer to specify the initial condition as the postcondition of an "initialization operation". In Object-Z, on the other hand, the role of each schema within a class and its order with respect to other schemas is strictly defined.

The second difference is that the principle of "definition before use" of Z does not always hold. It does not hold for class operations, which may be defined recursively. It also does not hold for variables whose values are object identities. Variables which reference objects of the specified system may be declared before the classes of those objects are defined. Not only does this allow greater flexibility when structuring specifications — for example, self and mutually recursive structures may be specified — it also enables different design strategies to be employed. For example, a system may be specified in a top-down fashion rather than by the usual bottom-up approach.

This chapter details the rules of scope and usage of constructs in Object-Z which determine the allowable forms of a specification. A formal syntax is given for each construct of Object-Z which is not also in Z using an extended BNF the extensions of which are described in Chapter 6. The goal of the chapter is to assist the understanding of the more rigorous descriptions of Object-Z in Chapters 4 and 6. These chapters provide respectively summaries of the descriptions given in this chapter along with rules of usage and semi-formal definitions, and a full syntax of Object-Z including those constructs also in Z.

3.1 Class Definitions

Object-Z introduces to Z only one new kind of formal paragraph — the class definition. A class definition captures the object-oriented notion of a class by encapsulating a single state schema with its initial state schema and all the operations which can affect its variables. Class definitions are the basic building blocks of specifications in Object-Z. They can be used to specify the state and operations of the objects which constitute a system, as well as the system, and its subsystems, in terms of references to such objects.

A class definition comprises a named box possibly with generic parameters. In this box there may be, in the order in which they can occur, a visibility list defining the class's interface (Section 3.2), inherited class designators (Section 3.3), local type and constant definitions (Section 3.4), at most one state schema (Section 3.5) and associated initial state schema (Section 3.6) and operations (Section 3.7). Each of these constructs is local to the class and hence may have names, where applicable, identical to constructs in other classes.

```
                 ┌─ ClassName [FormalParameters] ─────
Paragraph ::=    │ [VisibilityList]
                 │ [InheritedClass
                 │   ⋮
                 │  InheritedClass]
                 │ [LocalDefinition
                 │   ⋮
                 │  LocalDefinition]
                 │ [State]
                 │ [InitialState]
                 │ [Operation
                 │   ⋮
                 │  Operation]
                 └────────────────────────────────────
```

The header of a class definition comprises a class name and an optional list of formal generic parameters. The class name is a *word* — that is, either it comprises an upper or lower case letter followed by a sequence of letters, digits and underscores, or is a special symbol.

ClassName ::= Word

It is used to identify the class and, hence, must be distinct from all other global names appearing in the specification. That is, it must be distinct from the names of all global types and constants, schemas and other classes.

The formal generic parameters appear identically to those of generic schemas in Z — that is, as a square-bracketed and comma-separated list of identifiers. An identifier is word with an optional decoration. Decorations are, as in Z, sequences of the characters ′, ? and ! and subscript digits.

FormalParameters ::= [Identifier, ..., Identifier]

Each formal generic parameter effectively introduces a basic type whose scope comprises the constructs in the class box. It denotes a type whose value is not yet defined. Therefore, a generic parameter can only be used in an expression or predicate in which any possible type can be used. Similarly, constants and variables declared in terms of a generic parameter can only be used in expressions and predicates which are not type specific. For example, consider the following generic class $A[T]$.

$A[T]$

$x : T$
$y : \mathbb{P}\, T$

$x \in y$

Op

$\Delta(x)$
$x? : T$

$x? \in y$
$x' = x?$

The state variables x and y are defined in terms of the formal generic parameter T as is the input variable $x?$ of the operation Op. The state predicate $x \in y$ is valid for any instantiation of T. Similarly, the predicates of Op are valid for any instantiation of T. A predicate such as $x \in 0 \mathinner{\ldotp\ldotp} 10$, however, would not be valid unless T was instantiated by a type, such as the set of natural numbers, which included the numbers 0 to 10. Hence, such a predicate cannot appear in this class.

Generic parameters promote class reuse by reducing the need to specify almost identical classes. They are particularly useful for specifying classes representing data structures — such as queues, arrays and trees — whose behaviours are independent of their constituent elements. When a class is used — to define an expression (Section 3.9) or as an inherited class (Section 3.3) — its formal generic parameters must be replaced by actual generic parameters. These are expressions which define the types represented by the formal generic parameters and, hence, a particular instantiation of the class.

Each of the constructs which appear within the class box are optional. Hence, the simplest class with name B and no generic parameters is as below.

B

Generally, however, a class box will include at least one, and usually more than one, construct. These constructs are detailed in Sections 3.2 to 3.7.

3.2 Visibility Lists

The visibility list of a class defines the class's interface. It explicitly defines which features — constants, state variables, initial state schema and operations — are able to be referred to in the environment of an object of the class. It enables those features which are not external features of the class, but used to simplify the definitions of the external features, to be hidden. For example, an operation may be defined in terms of a number of simpler operations which themselves are not visible. It is also the only construct of a class which is not inherited. Hence, a subclass can change which features are visible enabling inherited features to be cancelled or redefined as detailed in Section 3.3.1.

The visibility list precedes all other constructs in a class. It is a bracketed and comma-separated list of identifiers preceded by the projection symbol $\upharpoonright$.

$$\mathsf{VisibilityList} ::= \upharpoonright(\mathsf{Identifier}, \ldots, \mathsf{Identifier})$$

Each identifier is the name of a class feature. When no visibility list is given in a class, all features are visible. To specify that no features are visible, the empty visibility list $\upharpoonright()$ must be explicitly included in the class box.

3.3 Inherited Classes

When a class is inherited by another in Object-Z its definitions — local definitions, state and initial state schemas, and operations — are *merged* with those of the inheriting class. That is, its definitions are either implicitly available in the inherited class or, when they have the same name as an explicit definition, implicitly identified or conjoined with this definition. It is not always possible, therefore, for one class to inherit another. Inheritance is only possible when all names common to the inherited and inheriting classes are used for the same kind of definitions — the name of an operation in one of the classes may not be the same as that of a state variable in the other for example — and the definitions themselves are compatible.

Inherited local types and constants are implicitly available to all definitions in the class. That is, their names may appear in the predicates and expressions of these definitions. Any types or constants with the same name occurring in both the inherited and inheriting class are semantically identified and hence must have compatible definitions. Two type definitions are compatible only when they define identical sets. Two constant definitions are compatible when the *base types* of the constants are the same. For example, $\mathbb{P}(X \times Y)$, where X and Y are basic types, is the base type of c in the declaration $c : X \leftrightarrow Y$. It is also, the base type of c in the declaration $c : X \rightarrow Y$. Hence, the declarations are compatible.

Base types are either basic types, including the types $\mathbb{Z}$ and $\mathbb{B}$ as well as the basic types and types associated with classes of the specification, or constructed from these basic types. The kinds of constructed types are set types, Cartesian product types, schema types, and, in the case of class types, polymorphic types constructed using class union. The base type of a type $\downarrow C$, where C is a class, is a class union type involving C and all of its subclasses.

The inherited class's state schema and initial state schema are implicitly conjoined with those defined explicitly in the inheriting class. Hence, common-named state variables are identified and must have compatible types as is required for schema conjunction.

An inherited operation whose name is distinct from those defined explicitly in the class is implicitly available to the operation definitions. When an inherited operation has the same name as an operation in the inheriting class, it is implicitly conjoined with that operation. Hence, common-named input and output variables of such operations must have compatible types.

It is important to note that conjoining an inherited operation Op with an operation Op in the inheriting class does not affect the meaning of other inherited operations which are defined in terms of Op. That is, these operations are still defined in terms of the inherited operation Op, not Op of the inheriting class. For example, if class A has operations Op_1, Op_2 and Op_3 and Op_3 is defined syntactically as $Op_1 \wedge Op_2$, changing the meaning of Op_1 in a subclass B of A does not change the meaning of Op_3 in B. This enables inheritance to be defined independently of the syntactic representation of the inherited class. If Op_3 were replaced with a semantically equivalent definition in A which did not refer to Op_1 then the meaning of B would be unchanged. It also follows that if A were to be replaced by a refinement then B, and any specification containing the classes A and B, would also be refined.

Inheritance is indicated in a class definition by the inclusion of inherited class designators. The inherited class designators appear after the visibility list but before all other constructs in a class definition. They comprise a class name, an instantiation of that class's generic parameters, if any, and possibly a rename list.

$$\mathsf{InheritedClass} ::= \mathsf{ClassName}\,\mathit{[}\mathsf{ActualParameters}\mathit{]}\ \mathit{[}\mathsf{RenameList}\mathit{]}$$

The class name must be that of a class which has been previously defined in the specification. Forward usage of class names applies only to their use as expressions (Section 3.9) and not to inheritance. For each formal generic parameter of the inherited class, the inherited class designator will have an actual generic parameter in a square-bracketed, comma-separated list.

$$\mathsf{ActualParameters} ::= [\mathsf{Expression}, \ldots, \mathsf{Expression}]$$

The actual generic parameters are expressions defined in terms of previously defined global types and constants, class names and, if the inheriting class is also generic, in terms of its formal generic parameters. Inheriting an instantiation of a generic class is identical to inheriting a class formed by textually substituting each occurrence of a formal generic parameter by its corresponding actual generic parameter. For example, inheriting the class $A[T]$ of Section 3.1 with T instantiated with $\mathbb{N}$ — that is, $A[\mathbb{N}]$ — is identical to inheriting the class $A1$ below.

*A*1

$x : \mathbb{N}$
$y : \mathbb{P}\,\mathbb{N}$

$x \in y$

Op

$\Delta(x)$
$x? : \mathbb{N}$

$x? \in y$
$x' = x?$

An inherited class designator may also have a rename list. Renaming enables names to be given to inherited features and variables declared in inherited operations which are more meaningful for the inheriting class. It also enables name clashes to be avoided when necessary. The rename list is syntactically identical to the rename list of a schema in Z — that is, a square-bracketed and comma-separated list of identifier pairs.

RenameList ::= [Identifier/Identifier, . . . , Identifier/Identifier]

Each pair of identifiers is of the form *new_name*/*old_name* where *old_name* is the name of either a feature of the inherited class or a variable declared in one of its operations, and *new_name* is the name to which it is to be renamed. In the case where a variable name occurs in the declaration of more than one operation, all occurrences are renamed.

Inheriting a renamed class is identical to inheriting a class formed by textually substituting each occurrence of an *old_name* by its corresponding *new_name*. For example, inheriting class *A*1 with x renamed to x_2, *Op* renamed to Op_2 and the input variable $x?$ of *Op* renamed to $x_2?$ — that is, $A1[x_2/x, Op_2/Op, x_2?/x?]$ — is identical to inheriting the class *A*2 below.

*A*2

$x_2 : \mathbb{N}$
$y : \mathbb{P}\,\mathbb{N}$

$x_2 \in y$

Op_2

$\Delta(x_2)$
$x_2? : \mathbb{N}$

$x_2? \in y$
$x_2' = x_2?$

A name can only appear as an *old_name* once in a rename list. A *new_name* can be used more than once or be the same as the name of a feature or operation variable of the inherited class. Any features which have the same name after renaming are identified and hence must also have identical types. Similarly, for any variables occurring in the same operation.

3.3.1 Cancellation and redefinition of features

The only construct of a class which is not inherited is the visibility list. The visibility list of the inheriting class is, therefore, totally independent of that of the inherited class. Hence, inherited features can be effectively cancelled — that is, removed from the class interface — and, through a combination of renaming and cancellation, redefined.

The merging of common-named attributes and common-named operations in the inherited and inheriting classes, enables limited redefinition. The constraints on the values which constants and state variables can take can be strengthened. Further input and output variables can be added to operations and pre- and postconditions can be strengthened.

Arbitrary redefinition of an inherited feature is effected by renaming the feature and then cancelling the renamed feature by not including it in the inheriting class's visibility list. For example, consider the following class $B[T]$ which inherits the class $A[T]$ of Section 3.1 and redefines the variable y to be a bag, rather than a set, of elements of type T.

$B[T]$

$\upharpoonright(x, y, Op)$

$A[y_1/y, Op_1/Op]$

$y : \text{bag}\ T$
$x \sqsubseteq y$

Op

$\Delta(x)$ $x? : T$
$x? \sqsubseteq y$ $x' = x?$

The class $A[T]$ is inherited by $B[T]$ with its state variable y renamed to y_1 and its operation Op renamed to Op_1. These features are not included in the class's visibility list and hence are effectively cancelled. The class defines a new state variable y which is a bag of elements of type T of which x is a member, and a new operation Op which changes x to another value in the bag y.

The interface of the class is identical to that of $A[T]$ and the state variable y and operation Op have been effectively redefined. Any feature of an inherited class can be redefined in the same way. Since, in this case, there is only one feature unaffected by the redefinition — namely x — the class could have just as easily been defined without using inheritance. In classes with many features, this is not always the case. Using inheritance also permits the inclusion of the inheriting class in polymorphic types defined using the polymorphism operator $\downarrow$.

3.4 Local Definitions

The local definitions of a class define types and constants which may be used within the class. They appear in a class definition after any inherited class designators and before the class's state schema, initial state schema and operations.

The syntax of the local definitions of a class is the same as that of non-generic global type and constant definitions in Z. All generic parameters required for the definitions must appear in the class header. The name of a local type or constant must be distinct from any names occurring before it in the class but may be the same as any other names occurring in other classes and globally. In the case where a local type or constant name is the same as a previously declared global name, for the extent of its scope, the local definition overrides the global definition.

3.4.1 Basic types

A local basic type definition introduces one or more basic types by the inclusion of their names in a square-bracketed, comma-separated list.

$$\mathsf{LocalDefinition} ::= [\mathsf{Identifier}, \ldots, \mathsf{Identifier}]$$

The scope of a local basic type extends from its definition to the end of the class. As with all local types, the value of a basic type is identical for all objects of the class. This is necessary so that such objects can communicate via input and output parameters declared in terms of such types.

3.4.2 Axiomatic definitions

A local axiomatic definition introduces one or more local constants by a list of declarations and an optional list of predicates constraining their values.

$$\mathsf{LocalDefinition} ::= \mathit{[}\ \begin{array}{|l} \mathsf{Declaration} \\ \hline \mathsf{PredicateList}\mathit{]} \end{array}$$

The scope of a local constant extends from the end of the declaration part of the axiomatic definition to the end of the class. Hence, as in Z, a constant may not be used in the declaration of another constant in the same axiomatic definition.

The value a constant may take is constrained by its declared type and the predicates of its axiomatic definition as well as the predicates of any axiomatic definition following it in the class and the predicates of the class's state and initial state schemas. The value of constants may differ for different objects of the class.

3.4.3 Abbreviation definitions

A local abbreviation definition introduces a type whose name is the identifier on the right-hand side of the definition and whose values are those of the expression on the left-hand side.

LocalDefinition ::= Identifier == Expression

The scope of a type introduced by a local abbreviation extends from its definition to the end of the class.

3.4.4 Free types

A local free type definition introduces a type whose name is the identifier on the left-hand side of the expression and whose values are given by the branches of the right-hand side of the definition. (The second occurrence of the symbol ::= is Object-Z syntax and not part of the BNF notation.)

LocalDefinition ::= Identifier ::= Branch | ... | Branch

A branch is an identifier followed by an optional expression enclosed in double angle brackets.

Branch ::= Identifier *[* ⟨⟨Expression⟩⟩ *]*

If a branch is just an identifier it represents a value of the free type. When a branch comprises an identifier and an expression, it represents a subset of the values of the free type. The identifier represents an injection — that is, a one-to-one function — whose domain is defined by the expression and whose range is the free type. The subset of values represented by the branch are those related to values in the expression by the injection. The values of the free type represented by each branch are distinct.

The scope of a free type includes its definition and extends to the end of its class. The expression of a branch may, therefore, refer to the name of the free type allowing recursive definitions. Such recursive definitions are interpreted as they are in Z — the interested reader is referred to J.M. Spivey's *The Z Notation* (Prentice Hall, 1989 & 1992).

3.5 State Schemas

The state schema defines the state variables of a class. Along with any local axiomatic definitions it defines the possible states of the class. Each of these states also includes an implicit constant *self* (Section 3.9.6) denoting the object's identity. When a class has no state schema and no local axiomatic definitions, each of its objects has a single state comprising only the constant *self*.

The state schema appears in a class definition after the local definitions and before the initial state schema and operations. It is a nameless box with either a declaration part and optional predicate part or just a predicate part. The declaration and predicate parts are separated by a horizontal line as in Z. The state schema's declaration part may also be partitioned by a Δ into primary and secondary variables.

```
State ::=    ┌────────────────────────
             │ Declaration
             │ [Δ
             │  Declaration]
          [  ├──────────
             │ PredicateList]
             └────────────────────────

      |      ┌────────────────────────
             │ Δ
             │ Declaration
          [  ├──────────
             │ PredicateList]
             └────────────────────────

      |      ┌────────────────────────
             │ PredicateList
             └────────────────────────
```

Primary variables may only be changed by an operation when they are included in the operation's Δ-list (see Section 3.7). Secondary variables, on the other hand, may be changed by any operation. Rather than representing an independent part of the state information, they are usually defined in terms of the primary variables and used as a convenient means of accessing derivable information. For example, the state schema of a "square" class may have *side* (denoting the length of a side) as a primary variable and *area* and *perim* (denoting the area and perimeter respectively) as secondary variables as shown below.

```
┌──────────────────────────────
│ side : ℕ
│ Δ
│ area, perim : ℕ
├──────────────
│ area = side * side
│ perim = 4 * side
└──────────────────────────────
```

The scope of a state variable extends from the end of the declaration part of the state schema to the end of the class. Hence, as in Z, a state variable may not be used in the declaration of another state variable.

A state variable's name must be distinct from that of any inherited or explicitly defined local definition but may be the same as names occurring in other classes or globally. In the case where the name of a state variable is the same as that of a previously declared global name, for the extent of its scope, the state variable overrides the global definition.

A state schema can also be defined in horizontal form.

$$
\begin{aligned}
\mathsf{State} ::= {} & \left[\mathsf{Declaration}\ \mathit{[}\Delta\ \mathsf{Declaration}\mathit{]}\ \mathit{[}\ |\ \mathsf{Predicate}\mathit{]}\right] \\
| {} & \left[\Delta\ \mathsf{Declaration}\ \mathit{[}\ |\ \mathsf{Predicate}\mathit{]}\right] \\
| {} & \left[\mathsf{Predicate}\right]
\end{aligned}
$$

For example, the state schema of the "square" class above could be written as follows.

$$\left[side : \mathbb{N}\ \ \Delta\ \ area, perim : \mathbb{N} \mid area = side * side \land perim = 4 * side\right]$$

3.6 Initial State Schemas

The initial state schema defines the initial states of a class. These are the possible states of the class that an object of the class which has not undergone any operations may be in. It appears after the state schema and before any operation definitions as a box with the special symbol *INIT* as its name. This symbol cannot be used for any other purpose in a specification.

```
                   _INIT______________________________
InitialState ::=  | PredicateList
                  |___________________________________
```

The initial state schema has no declaration part — the state variables and constants of the class are available in the environment in which it is interpreted. The predicates restrict the possible values of the state variables and constants of the class. They implicitly include the state schemas predicates and any predicates associated with the constant definitions. When a class has no initial state schema, the initial states of the class are any possible states of the class.

The initial state schema can also be defined in horizontal form.

$$\mathsf{InitialState} ::= \mathit{INIT} \mathrel{\widehat=} \left[\mathsf{Predicate}\right]$$

3.7 Operations

The operations of a class define the permissible changes in state that an object of the class may undergo. Together with the initial state schema they define the reachable states of the class — that is, the states which can be reached starting from an initial state and applying a sequence of operations. These are the only states of the class an object may be in.

The operations appear in a class definition after the initial state schema and are defined either by operation schemas (Section 3.7.1), operation promotions which model the application of an operation to an object referenced by the class (Section 3.7.2), or operations constructed from operation schemas and operation promotions using Object-Z's operation operators (Section 3.7.3 and Section 3.7.4). The environment in which operations are interpreted includes the constants and state variables of the class. This environment is enriched with the state variables of the class in primed form. The state schema's predicate in both primed and unprimed form along with any predicates associated with the constant definitions are implicitly included in each operation definition.

The scope of an operation includes its definition and extends to the end of the class. Its name must be distinct from any other name occurring before it in the class. It can be the same as a name occurring globally or in another class. In the case where the name of an operation is the same as that of a previously declared global name, for the extent of its scope the operation definition overrides the global definition.

3.7.1 Operation schemas

An operation schema is a named box in which there may be a Δ-list, a declaration part and a predicate part. Each part is optional allowing the entire definition of an operation to be *deferred*. That is, the operation's definition may be given only for subclasses of the class in which the operation occurs.

```
                 ┌─OperationName──────────────
Operation ::=    │ DeltaList
                 │ [Declaration]
               [ ├───────────
                 │ PredicateList]
                 └────────────────────────────

                 ┌─OperationName──────────────
            |    │ Declaration
               [ ├───────────
                 │ PredicateList]
                 └────────────────────────────

                 ┌─OperationName──────────────
            |    │ [PredicateList]
                 └────────────────────────────
```

An operation name is an identifier.

OperationName ::= Identifier

A Δ-list is a bracketed and comma-separated list of identifiers preceded by the symbol Δ.

$$\mathsf{DeltaList} ::= \Delta(\mathsf{Identifier}, \ldots, \mathsf{Identifier})$$

The identifiers are primary variables which the operation may change when it is applied to an object of the class — all other primary variables remain unchanged. The absence of a Δ-list in an operation schema is equivalent to having an empty Δ-list — that is, no primary variables can change.

The declarations are of auxiliary variables needed to define the operation. They are generally input and output variables but may also include other (possibly undecorated) variables. The scope of an auxiliary variable comprises only the operation schema's predicate part. Therefore, it may not be used in the declaration of another of the operation schema's variable declarations. The types of these variables may, however, be given in terms of the state variables of the class (in both primed and unprimed form) since these are available to the operation definition and not part of it. For example, the operation *Op* of the class A below outputs a value from the set denoted by the state variable s.

A

$$s : \mathbb{P}\,\mathbb{N}$$

Op

$$\Delta(s)$$
$$x! : s$$

$$s' = s \setminus \{x!\}$$

The name of an auxiliary variable must be distinct from the name of any inherited type or feature and any name explicitly declared before it in the class. It may be the same as a name declared globally, within another class or within another operation of its class. In the case where an auxiliary variable's name is the same as that of a previously declared global name, for the extent of its scope, the auxiliary variable overrides the global definition.

The predicates of an operation schema relate the possible states before the operation — denoted by the constants and unprimed state variables — to the possible states after the operation — denoted by the constants and primed state variables. The precondition implicit in an operation's predicate can be derived, as in Z, by existentially quantifying over the primed state variables and output variables of the operation. For example, the precondition of *Op* above is the following.

$$\exists s' : \mathbb{P}\,\mathbb{N};\ x! : s \bullet s' = s \setminus \{x!\}$$

An operation can only occur when its precondition is satisfied. When its precondition is not satisfied, the operation is said to be *blocked* — that is, it is not available for application. This is in contrast to Z where an operation may occur when its precondition is not satisfied — the result of the operation, in such cases, being undefined. There are two major consequences of this difference. Firstly, there is no need for the specifier to check that operations are sufficiently defined and, in the cases where they are not, combine them with appropriate error schemas. It is, however, important for the specifier to be aware that the operation definition is complete and explicitly add nondeterminism when required. Secondly, refinement of an operation by weakening its preconditions is generally not applicable. Instead, a new operation often needs to be introduced during refinement which, together with the original operation, provides the wider precondition.

An operation schema can also be defined in horizontal form.

Operation ::= OperationName $\widehat{=}$ OperationExpression

OperationExpression ::= [DeltaList *[*Declaration*]* *[* | Predicate*]*]
| [Declaration *[* | Predicate*]*]
| [*[*Predicate*]*]

For example, the operation *Op* above could have been written as follows.

$$Op \widehat{=} [\Delta(s)\ \ x! : s \mid s' = s \setminus \{x!\}]$$

3.7.2 Operation promotions

A system class which references a collection of objects can have, as well as operations which change its state, operations which model the application of operations to the objects it references. Such operations are said to *promote* the operations of the objects to operations of the class. An operation promotion is defined using the dot notation.

OperationExpression ::= Expression . Identifier *[*RenameList*]*

The expression evaluates to the identity of a referenced object and the identifier is the name of a visible operation of the object's class. The form of the rename list is as described at the beginning of Section 3.7.3.

Since the state variables in both primed and unprimed form are available to an operation, they may be used in the expression identifying the object. For example, the expression may be a state variable as in the class below. (*A* is the class defined in the previous section.)

C

$a : A$

$Op \widehat{=} a.Op$

As with other operations, an operation promotion has an associated Δ-list and auxiliary variables. Since it does not change any primary variables of the class in which it occurs the Δ-list is empty. The auxiliary variables are those of the operation applied to the object. These are declared implicitly in the promoted operation.

In the case of object identities declared using the polymorphism operator $\downarrow$ or class union, generally only operations in the *polymorphic core* — that is, operations belonging to all classes which constitute the type — may be promoted. Operations of a particular class which are not in the polymorphic core may only be promoted in a scope where the object in question is *qualified* to be of that class. This notion of qualification is discussed in Section 3.9.5.

3.7.3 Operation operators

Object-Z has a number of operation operators similar to the schema operators of Z. These operators are used to modify and combine operation expressions which include schema definitions and operation promotions. An operation expression may also be an identifier with an optional rename list enabling previously defined operations to be modified or combined.

$$\mathsf{OperationExpression} ::= \mathsf{Identifier}\,/\mathsf{RenameList}/$$

The identifier must be the name of an operation which has been inherited or previously defined in the class, or the name of the operation being defined. Recursive operation definitions are described in Section 3.7.5.

The rename list is a square-bracketed and comma-separated list of identifier pairs.

$$\mathsf{RenameList} ::= [\mathsf{Identifier}/\mathsf{Identifier}, \ldots, \mathsf{Identifier}/\mathsf{Identifier}]$$

Each pair of identifiers is of the form new_name/old_name where old_name is the name of an auxiliary variable of the identified operation and new_name is the name to which it is to be renamed. Attributes and primed state variables cannot be renamed as they are only available to the identified operation and not part of it.

There are six binary operation operators — conjunction $\wedge$, two kinds of parallel composition $\|$ and $\|_!$, nondeterministic choice $[]$, sequential composition $⨟$ and the scope enrichment operator $\bullet$ used to enrich the environment of one operation expression with the auxiliary variables of the other.

When two operation expressions are combined to define a new operation their Δ-lists are united so that the new operation can change any variable which either of its constituent operations could have changed. Operation expressions can only be combined when they are type compatible. That is, any auxiliary variables common to both operation expressions must have the same base type. The auxiliary variables of the resulting operation expression includes all of those from the arguments. The (base) types of these variables are the same as in the arguments.

There is also an operation operator for hiding auxiliary variables of operation expressions. The hiding operator binds more tightly than the binary operators which listed in decreasing order of binding power are $\wedge$, $\|$, $\|_!$, $[]$, $⨟$ and $\bullet$.

Conjunction

The conjunction operator $\wedge$ is a commutative and associative binary operator similar to the schema conjunction operator, also denoted by $\wedge$, of Z.

$$\mathsf{OperationExpression} ::= \mathsf{OperationExpression} \wedge \mathsf{OperationExpression}$$

It is used to model the simultaneous occurrence of two operations. For example, in the following class the operation $IncBoth$ has the same effect as the operations $IncX$ and $IncY$ occurring together. That is, $IncBoth$ increments both x and y.

A

$x, y : \mathbb{N}$

$IncX$
$\Delta(x)$
$x' = x + 1$

$IncY$
$\Delta(y)$
$y' = y + 1$

$IncBoth \mathrel{\widehat{=}} IncX \wedge IncY$

The operation $IncBoth$ of class A above is semantically identical to the operation schema $IncBoth$ below.

$IncBoth$
$\Delta(x, y)$
$x' = x + 1$
$y' = y + 1$

It is important to note that it is not always possible to express the operation resulting from the conjunction of two operation schemas in this way. When one of the operation schemas refers to a global constant and the other overrides that global constant with an auxiliary variable of the same name, the predicate of the first operation schema cannot be interpreted correctly in the presence of the declarations of the second.

Parallel composition

The parallel composition operators $\|$ and $\|_!$ are commutative binary operators similar to the (non-commutative) schema piping operator $\gg$ of Z. The $\|_!$ operator is associative and the $\|$ operator is not.

$$\text{OperationExpression} ::= \text{OperationExpression} \parallel \text{OperationExpression}$$
$$\mid \text{OperationExpression} \parallel_! \text{OperationExpression}$$

These operators are used to model communication between simultaneously occurring operations. They conjoin the operation expressions and, in addition, identify and equate input variables in either operation with output variables in the other operation having the same basenames — that is, apart from the ? or ! decorations. For example, if the operation Op_1 has an output variable $x!$ and the operation Op_2 has an input variable $x?$ then these variables are equated in the operation $Op_1 \parallel Op_2$. Similarly, if Op_1 has an input variable $y?$ and Op_2 has an output variable $y!$ these are equated in $Op_1 \parallel Op_2$. That is, communication occurs in both directions in contrast to the unidirectional communication of the piping operator of Z.

The identified input variables are hidden in the resulting operations. With the $\parallel$ operator, the identified output variables are also hidden. With the $\parallel_!$ operator, the output variables are not hidden and so may be equated with other input variables in subsequent parallel compositions. For example, in the following class the operation Op_3 has no auxiliary variables while the operation Op_4 has an output parameter $x!$.

```
┌─ B ──────────────────────────────
│ ┌────────────────────────────
│ │ n : ℕ
│ └────────────────────────────
│ ┌─ Op1 ──────────────────────
│ │ x! : ℕ
│ ├──────────
│ │ x! < n
│ └────────────────────────────
│ ┌─ Op2 ──────────────────────
│ │ Δ(n)
│ │ x? : ℕ
│ ├──────────
│ │ n' = n + x?
│ └────────────────────────────
│
│ Op3 ≙ Op1 || Op2
│ Op4 ≙ Op1 ||! Op2
└──────────────────────────────────
```

The operation Op_3 is semantically identical to the following operation schema.

```
┌─ Op3 ────────────────────────────
│ Δ(n)
├──────────
│ ∃ x : ℕ •
│     x < n ∧
│     n' = n + x
└──────────────────────────────────
```

The existentially quantified variable x denotes the communicated value — $x!$ of Op_1 and $x?$ of Op_2.

The operation Op_4 is semantically identical to the following operation schema.

$$\begin{array}{|l} \multicolumn{1}{l}{Op_4} \\ \hline \Delta(n) \\ x! : \mathbb{N} \\ \hline x! < n \\ n' = n + x! \\ \hline \end{array}$$

In this case, the input variable $x?$ of Op_2 is simply identified with the output variable $x!$ of Op_1 and the resulting operation.

Parallel composition is particularly useful for modelling inter-object communication and synchronization — by composing promotions of the objects' operations. This is discussed in more detail in Chapter 5.

Nondeterministic choice

The nondeterministic choice operator $[]$ is a commutative and associative binary operator similar to the disjunction operator $\vee$ of Z.

$$\mathsf{OperationExpression} ::= \mathsf{OperationExpression} \; [] \; \mathsf{OperationExpression}$$

It is used to model angelic choice between operations. When only one of the operations is enabled, that operation will occur. When both operations are enabled, the operation that occurs is chosen nondeterministically. As with the disjunction operator of Z, its is possible that both operations occur. However, this is often precluded when the operations have different Δ-lists. For example, in the following class which inherits class A above, $IncEither$ has the effect of either operation $IncX$ occurring or operation $IncY$ occurring but not both.

$$\begin{array}{|l} \multicolumn{1}{l}{A1} \\ \hline A \\ IncEither \mathrel{\widehat=} IncX \; [] \; IncY \\ \hline \end{array}$$

The operation $IncEither$ of class $A1$ is semantically identical to the operation schema $IncEither$ below.

$$\begin{array}{|l} \multicolumn{1}{l}{IncEither} \\ \hline \Delta(x, y) \\ \hline x' = x + 1 \wedge y' = y \\ \vee \\ y' = y + 1 \wedge x' = x \\ \hline \end{array}$$

That is, either x is incremented and y is unchanged since y is not in the Δ-list of $IncX$, or y is incremented and x is unchanged since x is not in $IncY$'s Δ-list.

The use of the nondeterministic choice operator is restricted to argument operations which have the same auxiliary variables. Hence, the resulting operation's input and output variables are independent of the argument operation which occurs.

Sequential composition
The sequential composition operator $\fatsemi$ is a binary operator similar to the schema sequential composition operator, also denoted by $\fatsemi$, of Z. In addition, it allows communication between the argument operations. The operator is not commutative. Also, because the communicated inputs and outputs are hidden, it is not associative.

$$\mathsf{OperationExpression} ::= \mathsf{OperationExpression} \fatsemi \mathsf{OperationExpression}$$

The sequential composition operator is used to model two operations occurring in sequence. The entire operation, however, is atomic and is only enabled when the first operation — that occurring on the left-hand side of the $\fatsemi$ — can occur and result in a state from which the second operation can occur. The output variables of the first operation are identified and equated with the input variables of the second operation having the same basenames. These identified input and output variables are hidden in the resulting operation. For example, consider the operation Op_5 in the following class which inherits class B above.

$B1$
B
$Op_5 \mathrel{\widehat=} Op_4 \fatsemi Op_2$

The operation Op_5 of class $B1$ is semantically identical to the following operation schema. The existentially quantified variables n_0 and x denote the value of the variable n after Op_4 and before Op_2, and the communicated value respectively.

Op_5
$\Delta(n)$

$$\exists n_0 : \mathbb{N};\ x : \mathbb{N} \bullet \\ \quad x < n \wedge \\ \quad n_0 = n + x \wedge \\ \quad n' = n_0 + x$$

Scope enrichment
The scope enrichment operator $\bullet$ is a binary operator used to introduce an additional level of scope within an operation. It is neither commutative nor associative.

$$\mathsf{OperationExpression} ::= \mathsf{OperationExpression} \bullet \mathsf{OperationExpression}$$

Its primary purpose is to enable operation promotion to objects whose identities are not directly available as an attribute or global constant. The scope of any variable declared in the operation expression on the left-hand side of the expression is extended to include the operation expression on the right-hand side. For example, consider the following class where B is the class defined previously.

C

$s : \mathbb{P}\, B$

$Op \mathrel{\widehat{=}} [b_1, b_2 : s \mid b_1 \neq b_2] \bullet b_1.Op_1 \parallel b_2.Op_2$

The operation Op models the parallel composition of two objects whose identities are in the set s undergoing the operations Op_1 and Op_2. The left-hand side of the definition introduces the identities of the objects, b_1 and b_2, and ensures that they are distinct. The right-hand side specifies the parallel composition using the introduced variables b_1 and b_2.

Hiding

The hiding operator is similar to the hiding operator of Z. The variables to be hidden appear as a bracketed and comma-separated list of identifiers.

$$\mathsf{OperationExpression} ::= \mathsf{OperationExpression} \setminus (\mathsf{Identifier}, \ldots, \mathsf{Identifier})$$

The identifiers must be the names of auxiliary variables declared in the operation expression. Constants and state variables in both unprimed and primed form cannot be hidden since they are only available to the operation and not part of it.

The resulting operation is identical to the argument operation except that the hidden variables are no longer accessible in its environment. For example, consider the following class which inherits class B defined previously.

$B2$

B

$Op_5 \mathrel{\widehat{=}} Op_2 \setminus (x?)$

The operation Op_5 of class $B2$ is semantically identical to the following operation schema.

Op_5

$\Delta(n)$

$\exists x? : \mathbb{N} \bullet n' = n + x?$

In general, the Δ-list of the resulting operation expression is the same as that of the argument operation expression. The auxiliary variables of the resulting operation expression are those of the argument operation expression other than the hidden variables. Their types are the same as in the argument operation expression.

3.7.4 Distributed operators

Object-Z has three distributed operation operators based on the binary operators $\wedge$, $[]$ and $\fatsemi$. They are used to apply these operators to a collection of similar operation expressions when this collection is either large — and, therefore, the use of the binary forms of the operators is unwieldy — or of arbitrary size — and, therefore, the use of the binary forms of the operators is not possible. In the case of $\bigwedge$ and $[]$, they can also be used to apply these operators to an infinite set of operation expressions.

The collection of operation expressions to which the operators are applied are those formed by evaluating a given operation expression for each set of values assignable to a given declaration and satisfying a given predicate.

$$
\begin{aligned}
\mathsf{OperationExpression} ::= {} & \bigwedge \mathsf{Declaration} \,[\, | \,\mathsf{Predicate}] \bullet \mathsf{OperationExpression} \\
| {} & [] \;\mathsf{Declaration} \,[\, | \,\mathsf{Predicate}] \bullet \mathsf{OperationExpression} \\
| {} & \fatsemi \;\mathsf{Declaration} \,[\, | \,\mathsf{Predicate}] \bullet \mathsf{OperationExpression}
\end{aligned}
$$

The scope of a variable in the declaration comprises the predicate and operation expression. The types of these variables may be given in terms of the state variables of the class in both primed and unprimed form.

The name of a variable in the declaration must be distinct from the name of any auxiliary variable of the operation expression. In the case of the distributed sequential composition operator, the basename of any primed variable in the declaration must be distinct from the name of any undecorated variable of the operation expression. The variable names in the declaration need not, however, be distinct from the names of inherited types or features, or names explicitly declared before them in the class. Also. they may be the same as a name declared globally, within another class or within another operation of its class. In the case where a variable name in the declaration is the same as that of an inherited or explicitly declared type or feature, or of a previously declared global name, for the extent of its scope, it overrides the other definition.

As an example, consider the following class where B is the class defined previously.

D

$$s : \mathbb{P}\, B$$

$$Op_1 \mathrel{\widehat=} \bigwedge b : s \bullet b.Op_2$$

$$Op_2 \mathrel{\widehat=} [] \; b : s \mid b.n < 10 \bullet b.Op_2$$

$$Op_3 \mathrel{\widehat=} \fatsemi \; b : s \mid b.n < 10 \bullet b.Op_2$$

The operation Op_1 of class D models each of the objects of class B whose identity is in the set s undergoing the operation Op_2. For example, if s was the set $\{x, y, z\}$ where x, y and z were global constants of type B, then Op_1 would be semantically identical to the following operation.

$$Op_1 \mathrel{\widehat=} x.Op_2 \wedge y.Op_2 \wedge z.Op_2$$

Operation expressions involving the distributed conjunction operator can always be expressed in this expanded form except when there is an infinite set of values assignable to the declaration — for example, when s is infinite in class D.

The operation Op_2 of class D models an angelic choice of the objects of class B whose identity is in the set s and whose n attribute has a value less than 10 undergoing operation Op_2. For example, if s was the set $\{x, y, z\}$ where x, y and z were global constants of type B such that $x.n$ and $y.n$ were less than 10 and $z.n$ was greater than 10, then Op_2 would be semantically identical to the following operation.

$$Op_2 \mathrel{\widehat{=}} x.Op_2 \mathbin{[\!]} y.Op_2$$

Operation expressions involving the distributed choice operator can also always be expressed in this expanded form except when there is an infinite set of values assignable to the declaration.

The operation Op_3 of class D models each object of class B whose identity is in the set s and whose n attribute has a value less than 10 undergoing the operation Op_2 in turn. The order in which the objects undergo the operation is arbitrary. For example, if s was the set $\{x, y, z\}$ where x, y and z were global constants of type B and $x.n$ and $y.n$ were less than 10 and $z.n$ was greater than 10, then Op_2 would be semantically identical to the following operation.

$$Op_3 \mathrel{\widehat{=}} (x.Op_2 \fatsemi y.Op_2) \mathbin{[\!]} (y.Op_2 \fatsemi x.Op_2)$$

In this case, the order doesn't make a difference and, in fact, the sequential composition is identical to conjunction since the composed operations affect distinct objects. Sequential composition is more useful when one or more objects is affected by subsequent composed operations. For example, consider the following class $D1$ which inherits class D above.

$D1$

D

$b_1 : B$

$b_1 \in s$

$Op_4 \mathrel{\widehat{=}} \fatsemi\, b_2 : s \mid b_2 \neq b_1 \bullet b_2.Op_1 \parallel b_1.Op_2$

The operation Op_4 of $D1$ models an object of class B whose identity is in the set s — denoted by the state variable b_1 — undergoing operation Op_2 in parallel with each other object of class B whose identity is in s, in turn, undergoing operation Op_1. That is, the object identified by b_1 is affected by every operation in the sequential composition.

When there is an infinite set of values assignable to the declaration of a distributed sequential composition, there is, in general, no possible postcondition — since there is no state representing the termination of the sequence of operations. Hence, the precondition, which requires the existence of a postcondition, is false and such an operation can never occur.

3.7.5 Recursion

A recursive operation definition is one in which the operation expression defining the operation is given in terms of the operation it is defining. The operation's name may appear as the applied operation in an operation promotion or as an argument to an operation operator. Operation names, unlike Z schema names, cannot occur in the declarations and predicates of operation schemas.

Recursive operation definitions risk being circular and, hence, having no real meaning. Such circular definitions are interpreted as having a false precondition — that is, they can never occur. For example, consider the following class A.

$$
\begin{array}{|l}
\multicolumn{1}{l}{A} \\
\hline
\quad n : \mathbb{N} \\
\\
Op_1 \mathrel{\widehat=} [\Delta(n) \mid n' = n + 1] \mathbin{;} Op_1 \\
Op_2 \mathrel{\widehat=} ([\Delta(n) \mid n' = n + 1] \mathbin{;} Op_2) \\
\qquad\quad [\!] \\
\qquad\quad [n > 10] \\
\hline
\end{array}
$$

The recursion in the operation Op_1 of class A never terminates. Each occurrence of operation Op_1 involves another occurrence of Op_1. Such an operation has a false precondition and, therefore, is not really useful in a specification.

The recursion in the operation Op_2, on the other hand, can terminate whenever the value of the state variable n is greater than 10. The operation increments n a nondeterministic number of times before terminating with $n > 10$. That is, it is semantically identical to the following operation.

$$Op_2 \mathrel{\widehat=} [\!]\ i : \mathbb{N} \bullet [\Delta(n) \mid n' = n + i \wedge n' > 10]$$

A general technique for constructing an operation which is semantically identical to a recursively defined operation involves transforming the recursive operation definition into a non-recursive function whose domain and range values are operations. For example, the recursive definition of Op_2 in class A is transformed into the following function ϕ.

$$\phi = \lambda x \bullet ([\Delta(n) \mid n' = n + 1] \mathbin{;} x)\ [\!]\ [n > 10]$$

An occurrence of Op_2 which terminates without any recursion is semantically identical to an occurrence of the operation denoted by $\phi([\text{false}])$.

$$
\begin{aligned}
\phi([\text{false}]) &= ([\Delta(n) \mid n' = n + 1] \mathbin{;} [\text{false}])\ [\!]\ [n > 10] \\
&= [n > 10]
\end{aligned}
$$

That is, an occurrence of Op_2 without recursion is identical to an occurrence of an operation which does not change n but requires (as a precondition) that n is greater than 10.

An occurrence of Op_2 which terminates after at most one recursion is semantically identical to an occurrence of the operation denoted by $\phi(\phi([\text{false}]))$.

$$\begin{aligned}\phi(\phi([\text{false}])) &= \phi([n > 10]) \\ &= ([\Delta(n) \mid n' = n+1] \mathbin{⨾} [x > 10]) \mathbin{[]} [n > 10] \\ &= [\Delta(n) \mid n' = n+1 \wedge n' > 10] \mathbin{[]} \phi([\text{false}])\end{aligned}$$

Continuing in this fashion, and noting that the operation expression $[n > 10]$ resulting from $\phi([\text{false}])$ is semantically identical to $[\Delta(n) \mid n' = n+0 \wedge n' > 10]$, we can deduce a general form for $\phi^{i+1}([\text{false}])$ (where i is any natural number). That is, we can deduce a general form for an operation which is semantically identical to an occurrence of Op_2 which terminates after at most i recursions.

$$\phi^{i+1}([\text{false}]) = [\Delta(n) \mid n' = n+i \wedge n' > 10] \mathbin{[]} \phi^{i}([\text{false}])$$

An operation semantically identical to Op_2 is given by the limit as i approaches infinity of $\phi^{i}([\text{false}])$. This limit can be expressed as follows.

$$limit_{i \to \infty}\ \phi^{i}([\text{false}]) = \mathop{[]}\ i : \mathbb{N} \bullet [\Delta(n) \mid n' = n+i \wedge n' > 10]$$

This technique can be used to interpret any recursive operation definition. For example, Op_1 of class A can be similarly transformed into the following function.

$$\chi = \lambda x \bullet [\Delta(n) \mid n' = n+1] \mathbin{⨾} x$$

The successive application of χ to the operation $[\text{false}]$ produces the following results.

$$\chi([\text{false}]) = [\Delta(n) \mid n' = n+1] \mathbin{⨾} [\text{false}] = [\text{false}]$$

$$\chi(\chi([\text{false}])) = [\Delta(n) \mid n' = n+1] \mathbin{⨾} [\text{false}] = [\text{false}]$$

$$\chi^{i+1}([\text{false}]) = [\text{false}], \quad \text{for all } i \in \mathbb{N}$$

The limit of $\chi^{i}([\text{false}])$ as i approaches infinity is simply the schema $[\text{false}]$. Therefore, the recursive definition of Op_1 in A is semantically identical to the following operation definition.

$$Op_1 \mathrel{\widehat{=}} [\text{false}]$$

As another example involving operation promotion consider the class B below.

```
┌─ B ─────────────────────────────────────────
│ ┌───────────────────────────────────────────
│ │ b : B
│ │ n : ℕ
│ └───────────────────────────────────────────
│
│ Op ≙ b.Op [] [Δ(n) | n' = n + 1]
└─────────────────────────────────────────────
```

The operation Op of class B will either increment the state variable n or apply Op to the object of class B identified by the state variable b. To construct a semantically identical non-recursive operation in this case requires first transforming B to a semantically identical class definition.

B

$\upharpoonright(b, n, Op)$

$b : B$
$n : \mathbb{N}$
Δ
$s : \mathbb{N} \to B$

$s(0) = self$
$\forall i : \mathbb{N} \bullet s(i).b = s(i+1)$

$False$

false

$Increment$

$\Delta(n)$

$n' = n + 1$

$Op \mathrel{\widehat=} b.Op \mathbin{[]} Increment$

This definition of B introduces a secondary variable s — modelling the infinite sequence of object references $self$, b, $b.b$, $b.b.b$, $\ldots$ — and two operations $False$ and $Increment$. These features are not in the class's visibility list and hence do not affect B's interface. The recursive operation Op can be transformed into the following function.

$$\psi = \lambda x \bullet b.x \mathbin{[]} Increment$$

Rather than applying ψ to $[\text{false}]$, we apply it to the semantically identical operation $False$. This is necessary so that the result of the function application is a syntactically valid operation expression.

$$\psi(False) = b.False \mathbin{[]} Increment = Increment$$

$$\psi(\psi(False)) = b.Increment \mathbin{[]} Increment$$

$$\psi^{i+1}(False) = s(i).Increment \mathbin{[]} \psi^{i}(False), \quad \text{for all } i \in \mathbb{N}$$

Op is semantically identical to the limit as i approaches infinity of $\psi^{i}(False)$. That is, its definition in B is semantically identical to the following.

$$Op \mathrel{\widehat=} \mathop{[]}\ i : \mathbb{N} \bullet s(i).Increment$$

The technique illustrated by the examples above is representative of a general technique of fixed-point theory for interpreting recursive definitions — the non-recursive definitions of the operations are the least fixed points of the operations' representative functions. The technique requires that the function representing the recursive definition is continuous and that there exists a complete partial order on its domain — that is, a partial order on its domain which has a least upper bound for all subsets of its domain and a minimum member.

The complete partial order required for Object-Z operations $\leqslant$ is defined below (A and B are any operations).

$$\left[\text{false}\right] \leqslant A$$
$$A \leqslant A \mathbin{[\!]} B$$
$$A \leqslant \left[\, true \,\right]$$

The least upper bound for a set s of operations is $\mathop{[\!]}\, x : s \bullet x$. The minimum member is $\left[\text{false}\right]$. The proof of continuity of functions such as ϕ, χ and ψ above is straightforward but not included in this book.

3.8 Predicates

Two new kinds of predicates are introduced in Object-Z — Boolean-valued expressions and predicates that state that an object is in an initial state.

3.8.1 Boolean-valued expressions

A new basic type $\mathbb{B}$ is introduced in Object-Z to enable the declaration of variables constructed from Boolean values. A Boolean value is a logical value — that is, it is either true or false. Therefore, an expression which evaluates to a Boolean value can be used as a predicate.

Predicate ::= Expression

For example, consider the following class A. The operation *Op* of A can occur whenever the Boolean-valued variable a is true. After the operation, a is false.

```
┌─ A ──────────────────────────────
│ ┌────────────────────────────
│ │ a : 𝔹
│ └────────────────────────────
│
│ ┌─ Op ────────────────────────
│ │ Δ(a)
│ ├──────────
│ │ a
│ │ ¬ a′
│ └────────────────────────────
└──────────────────────────────────
```

Boolean-valued expressions can also be used in the same ways as other expressions — given $a, b : \mathbb{B}$, for example, $a = b$ is a valid predicate. It is important to note, however, that $a = \text{true}$ and $a = \text{false}$ are not valid predicates — true and false are predicates in Z, not expressions. The correct way to express the value of a Boolean-valued variable a is by $a \Leftrightarrow \text{true}$ or $a \Leftrightarrow \text{false}$, or simply by a or $\neg\, a$.

3.8.2 Promoted initial state predicates

The initial state predicate of a class whose initial state schema is visible may be promoted to any scope in which an object identity of the class may be referenced. The promoted predicate states that the identified object is in an initial state. The promotion is specified using the dot notation $a.\mathit{INIT}$ where a is an expression which evaluates to the identity of the object.

$$\mathsf{Predicate} ::= \mathsf{Expression}.\mathit{INIT}$$

For example, consider the following class A which has a state variable a identifying an object of the class.

```
┌─ A ─────────────────────────────
│ ┌───────────────────────────
│ │ a : A
│ │ n : ℕ
│ └───────────────────────────
│
│ ┌─ INIT ────────────────────
│ │ n = 0
│ └───────────────────────────
│
│ ┌─ Op ──────────────────────
│ │ Δ(n)
│ ├──────────
│ │ a.INIT
│ │ n' = n + 1
│ └───────────────────────────
└─────────────────────────────────
```

The operation Op of A increments the state variable n. It can only occur when the object identified by the state variable a is in its initial state — that is, the state variable n of the object identified by a is equal to 0. It is semantically identical to the following schema.

```
┌─ Op ─────────────────────────────
│ Δ(n)
├──────────
│ a.n = 0
│ n' = n + 1
└──────────────────────────────────
```

The predicate $a.\mathit{INIT}$ evaluates to true when the object identified by a has not yet undergone any operations or has undergone one or more operations and returned to a state satisfying the initial state predicate of its class.

It is important to note that this notation cannot be used in an operation to define the post-state of an object. The notation $a'.\mathit{INIT}$ refers to the pre-state values of the object referenced by a' — that is, for the class A above it is semantically identical to $a'.n = 0$. The notation $a.\mathit{INIT}'$ is not valid.

Recursion
Consider replacing the initial state schema in the class A above with the following recursively defined initial state schema.

$$\begin{array}{|l} \hline \mathit{INIT} \\ \hline n = 0 \land a.\mathit{INIT} \\ \hline \end{array}$$

As with operations, recursive definitions of initial state schemas risk being circular and, hence, having no real meaning. Such circular definitions are interpreted as having a true predicate — that is, they place no constraints on the initial states of the class.

A general technique, similar to that described for operations in Section 3.7.5, can be used for constructing an initial state schema which is semantically identical to one defined recursively. Firstly, the class in which the definition occurs must be extended with a Boolean-valued constant b which is true. The recursive definition is then transformed into a non-recursive function whose domain and range values are initial state schemas. For example, the initial state schema above is transformed into the following function ϕ.

$$\phi = \lambda x \bullet [n = 0 \land a.x]$$

The initial state schema is semantically identical to that given by the limit as i approaches infinity of $\phi^i(b)$.

$$\phi(b) = [n = 0 \land a.b] = [n = 0]$$

$$\phi(\phi(b)) = [n = 0 \land a.n = 0]$$

Hence, the initial state schema above is semantically identical to the following.

$$[\forall s : \mathbb{N} \to A \mid s(0) = \mathit{self} \land (\forall i : \mathbb{N} \bullet s(i).a = s(i+1)) \bullet$$
$$\forall i : \mathbb{N} \bullet s(i).n = 0]$$

Note that the expression $\mathit{self}.n$ is equivalent to n.

3.9 Expressions

Object-Z introduces two new kinds of types — those corresponding to the object identities of a single class and those constructed from the object identities of a collection of classes using the polymorphism operator $\downarrow$ and class union $\cup$. Additional expressions are introduced which represent these types and refer to their instances.

3.9.1 Class names

A class name can be used as an expression and evaluates to the set of identities of objects of the class. This set is either countably infinite or, when the class has no initial states, empty. The latter occurs when the class's initial state predicate evaluates to false, or the class has no initial state schema and its state schema's predicate or a predicate associated with a constant definition evaluates to false.

The class name is followed by an instantiation of the class's generic parameters, if any, and possibly a rename list.

$$\mathsf{Expression} ::= \mathsf{ClassName}\,[\mathsf{ActualParameters}]\;[\mathsf{RenameList}]$$

The class name must be that of a class in the specification. It is possible that the expression occurs prior to the class's definition. In such cases the usage of the class name is referred to as *forward* usage. Such usage facilitates the specification of recursive structures and enables systems to be specified in a top-down fashion.

Each formal generic parameter of the class is replaced by an actual generic parameter in a fashion identical to that described for inherited class designators (Section 3.3). The actual generic parameters appear in a square-bracketed, comma-separated list. They are defined by expressions which may refer to any names, including those of any formal generic parameter, whose scope includes the class name expression.

$$\mathsf{ActualParameters} ::= [\mathsf{Expression}, \ldots, \mathsf{Expression}]$$

Renaming enables more meaningful names to be given to the visible features and auxiliary variables of visible operations of particular instances of a class. The rename list is a square-bracketed, comma-separated list of identifier pairs.

$$\mathsf{RenameList} ::= [\mathsf{Identifier}/\mathsf{Identifier}, \ldots, \mathsf{Identifier}/\mathsf{Identifier}]$$

Each pair of identifiers is of the form *new_name/old_name* where *old_name* is the name of a visible feature of the class or an auxiliary variable of one of its visible operations and *new_name* is the name to which it is to be renamed. Each *old_name* is replaced by its corresponding *new_name* in a fashion identical to that described for inherited class designators (Section 3.3).

A name can only appear as an *old_name* once in a rename list but can appear as a *new_name* more than once provided that any features or variables of the same operation which have the same name after renaming also have identical types.

It is important to note that renaming does not introduce a new type — the set of object identities of $A[y/x]$, where A is a class with a feature or auxiliary variable x, is identical to that of A. Renaming simply introduces new names for referring to particular visible features of the class.

3.9.2 Polymorphism

The polymorphism operator $\downarrow$ facilitates the specification of systems using traditional, inheritance-based polymorphism. It is used to define the set of object identities of a given class together with the object identities of all classes derived, either directly or indirectly, from that given class via inheritance. (Examples of the use of the polymorphism operator are given in Chapter 1.)

$$\mathsf{Expression} ::= \downarrow\mathsf{Expression}$$

The expression following the $\downarrow$ is a class name followed by an instantiation of its formal generic parameters, if any, and possibly a rename list. The syntax and interpretation of the actual generic parameters and rename list are as described for class name expressions above.

The class name must be that of a class in the specification and may occur either before or after the expression. All subclasses of the class — that is, those classes derived either directly or indirectly via inheritance and occurring either before or after the expression — must have the same formal generic parameters as the class and include, for each visible feature of the class, an identically named visible feature. Furthermore, these common-named visible features must be type compatible and, in the case of operations, have identical auxiliary variables. Type compatibility of constants and state variables was described in Section 3.3 and type compatibility of operations was described in Section 3.7.3.

The restriction on the subclasses ensures that each can be used in the same way as the given class. In particular, any expression applicable to an object of the given class is also applicable to objects of each of the subclasses. Any expression valid for an object of the given class is hence valid for an object of the polymorphic type. Expressions which are valid for objects of particular subclasses but not for the given class are not valid for objects of the polymorphic type unless the type of these objects is further *qualified*. This is discussed in Section 3.9.5 below.

3.9.3 Class union

Class union enables the definition of a set comprising the object identities of a collection of classes. It is a more general form of polymorphism than that of the polymorphism operator $\downarrow$ since the classes need not be related by inheritance nor have any restrictions on their features. The expression constructs a set of object identities which is the union of the sets of identities of its constituent classes. Like set union, class union is commutative and associative.

$$\mathsf{Expression} ::= \mathsf{Expression} \cup \mathsf{Expression}$$

Each constituent expression of a class union is either a class union expression or a class name followed by an instantiation of its formal generic parameters, if any, and possibly a rename list. The syntax and interpretation of the actual generic parameters and rename list are as for a class name expression.

The class names must be of classes in the specification and may occur either before or after the expression. The classes need not be related at all. However, expressions involving object identities of a class union type are only valid when they are valid for object identities of each constituent class of the class union expression, or when the class of the object identity is further *qualified*. This is discussed in Section 3.9.5 below.

3.9.4 Object containment

The object containment notation facilitates the specification of systems where objects are "contained" within others — that is, where objects are uniquely associated with another object of which they are conceptually a component. This notion can be used to restrict access to objects since they can only be directly contained by one object. An object can be indirectly contained by another object — when the other object contains the object's containing object — and can be referenced by any object. However, direct containment is unique. (An example of the use of object containment is given in Chapter 2.)

$$\mathsf{Expression} ::= \mathsf{Expression}_{©}$$

The expression preceding the © subscript is a class name followed by an instantiation of its formal generic parameters, if any, and possibly a rename list. The syntax and interpretation of the actual generic parameters and rename list are as for a class name expression.

The containment expression does not introduce a new type — the type $A_{©}$, where A is a class, is identical to the type A (both represent the same set of object identities). However, implicitly associated with $A_{©}$ is a global predicate which restricts distinct declarations of this type from having the same value and a global predicate which prevents an object either directly or indirectly containing itself.

3.9.5 Promoted attributes

The visible attributes of an object may be promoted to any scope in which that object's identity may be referenced. This is done using the dot notation.

$$\mathsf{Expression} ::= \mathsf{Expression.Identifier}$$

The expression on the left-hand side of the dot must evaluate to a variable whose type is the set of object identities of a single class or the set of object identities of a collection of classes (formed either by the polymorphism operator or class union). In the former case, the identifier on the right-hand side of the dot is the name of a visible attribute of the class. In the latter case, the identifier on the right-hand side of the dot must, in general, be the name of a visible attribute in the *polymorphic core* of the collection of classes. The polymorphic core is the set of features — attributes and operations — common to all objects in a polymorphic collection. For those collections of classes formed using the polymorphism operator, the polymorphic core is simply the set of attributes (and operations) of the root class of the hierarchy (see Section 3.9.2).

The values which constitute a polymorphic type are the union of those which constitute each of its constituent class types. Hence, it is possible to compare such types — for example, in predicates such as $A \subseteq A \cup B$. It is also possible to indicate that a variable of a polymorphic type belongs to a particular constituent class of that type. For example, given the declaration $a : A \cup B$, the predicate $a \in A$ is valid. We say that a is *qualified* by this predicate to be an identity of class A.

Any visible features of such a class A can be promoted within a scope where a variable of the polymorphic type is qualified to be of that class. For example, if class A has attribute $x : \mathbb{N}$ and class B does not then, given the declaration $a : A \cup B$, the predicate $a.x = 10$ is valid in any scope where a is qualified to be of class A — for example, the operation expression $[\, a \in A \,] \bullet [\, a.x = 10 \,]$ is valid.

3.9.6 Self

Each class has an implicit constant *self* whose value is an object identity of the class. The value of this constant for a given object is the identity of that object. Hence, it is used for specifying objects which reference themselves. (An example of the use of *self* is given in Chapter 2.)

Expression ::= *self*

The constant *self* can be used in the same way as any other constant of a class. However, it never appears in the class's visibility list — it is implicitly visible — it is not inherited, and it cannot be renamed. *self* is a reserved word and cannot be used for any other purpose.

4

Language Definition

This chapter provides a reference manual for the Object-Z language. It is intended to be kept on hand when using the language for clarification and reinforcement of the meaning and use of Object-Z constructs. The chapter includes a "manual page" for each of the syntactic constructs introduced in Chapter 3. Each manual page comprises a brief description of the construct, its concrete syntax, its type rules and other rules of usage — stated informally in English text — and a semi-formal definition of the construct in a simple meta-language.

The meta-language enables each Object-Z construct to be defined in terms of constructs of Z which intuitively capture its meaning. The definitions are stated in terms of *meta-variables* representing syntactic constructs of Object-Z, and *meta-functions* which relate meta-variables. The meta-variables are not explicitly declared in the definitions. Rather, the following naming conventions are adopted and used throughout the chapter.

A, B	classes
X	generic types
VL	visibility lists
LD	local definitions
ST	state schemas
IN	initial state schemas
Op	operation names
OP	operations
S, T	schemas
d	declarations
p, q	predicates
s, t	expressions
a, b	object references
x, y, z	variables

Predicates denoted by p and q are in fully expanded form — that is, they do not include schema references including *INIT*.

The meta-functions are denoted by names in bold print — for example, **visible** is a meta-function that returns the set of names of visible features of a class it is applied to. We begin the chapter by providing a complete list of the meta-functions and their meanings.

4.1 Meta-Functions

The meta-language used in this chapter uses a set of meta-functions to facilitate the expression of the meaning of Object-Z constructs in a semi-formal way. Each meta-function maps a subset of syntactic constructs of Object-Z to syntactic constructs of Z. They enable complex constructs to be decomposed into simpler ones. For example, an Object-Z operation can be decomposed into a Z schema and a set of variables representing the Δ-list. These components of an operation can then be used, for example, to give the meaning of applying that operation to an object. Below we provide complete lists of the meta-functions that can be applied to particular constructs.

The meta-functions that can be applied to a class are

visible which returns the set of names of visible features,
inherited which returns the set of inherited classes,
types which returns the set of names of local types,
state which returns a Z schema representing the state, and
init which returns a Z schema representing the initial state.

Also, given a name *Op* of an operation of a class, **Op** is a meta-function which returns a tuple comprising a set of variables representing the contribution to the Δ-list of the operation — in addition to that of any inherited operations of the same name — and a Z schema representing the contribution to the schema of the operation.

The only meta-function that can be applied to a visibility list is

visible which returns the set of names of features in the list.

The meta-functions that can be applied to a local definition are

types which returns the set of names of declared types, and
state which returns a Z schema representing the contribution to the state of the class. The contribution of local definitions is of the form of constant declarations and predicates constraining constants and types.

The meta-functions that can be applied to a state schema are

state which returns a Z schema representing the contribution to the state of the class, and
secondary which returns the set of secondary variables.

The only meta-function that can be applied to an initial state schema is

init which returns a Z schema representing the contribution to the initial state of the class.

The meta-functions that can be applied to an operation are

schema which returns a Z schema representing the operation,
delta-list which returns the set of variables in the operation's Δ-list,
inputs which returns the set of basenames of input variables, and
outputs which returns the set of basenames of output variables.

The meta-language also has two meta-functions which can be applied to Z constructs — that is, to schemas, declarations, predicates and expressions. The first, **vars**, returns the set of variables declared in a schema or declaration. It is defined as follows. (The definitions for schema expressions can be deduced from the definition for their expanded form.)

$$\begin{aligned}
&\mathbf{vars}([\, d \mid p \,]) = \mathbf{vars}(d)\\
&\mathbf{vars}(d_1;\ d_2) = \mathbf{vars}(d_1) \cup \mathbf{vars}(d_2)\\
&\mathbf{vars}(x_1, \ldots, x_n : t) = \{x_1, \ldots, x_n\}
\end{aligned}$$

The second meta-function **subs** is an infix function used for substituting syntactic constructs corresponding to expressions with other syntactic constructs corresponding to expressions. The substitution can be made to a schema, declaration, predicate or expression and applies to all expressions in the construct except names of bound variables. For example,

$$[a.x/x, a.y/y, a.z/z]\ \mathbf{subs}\ (\forall x : z \bullet x \in y)$$

is $\forall x : a.z \bullet x \in a.y$. There is no guarantee that the result of substitution is well-formed.

The meta-function **subs** is defined as follows. (The definitions for schema expressions can be deduced from the definition for their expanded form. Only indicative examples of substitution into predicates and expressions are given.)

$$\begin{aligned}
&[x/y]\ \mathbf{subs}\ [\, d \mid p \,] = [[x/y]\ \mathbf{subs}\ d \mid [x/y]\ \mathbf{subs}\ p\,] \quad \text{if } x \notin \mathbf{vars}(d)\\
&\qquad = [[x/y]\ \mathbf{subs}\ d \mid p\,] \quad \text{if } x \in \mathbf{vars}(d)\\
&[x/y]\ \mathbf{subs}\ (d_1;\ d_2) = [x/y]\ \mathbf{subs}\ d_1;\ [x/y]\ \mathbf{subs}\ d_2\\
&[x/y]\ \mathbf{subs}\ (x_1, \ldots, x_n : t) = x_1, \ldots, x_n : [x/y]\ \mathbf{subs}\ t\\
&[x/y]\ \mathbf{subs}\ (\forall\, d \mid p \bullet q) = \forall [x/y]\ \mathbf{subs}\ d \mid [x/y]\ \mathbf{subs}\ p \bullet [x/y]\ \mathbf{subs}\ q\\
&\qquad \text{if } x \notin \mathbf{vars}(d)\\
&\qquad = \forall [x/y]\ \mathbf{subs}\ d \mid p \bullet q \quad \text{if } x \in \mathbf{vars}(d)\\
&[x/y]\ \mathbf{subs}\ (p \land q) = [x/y]\ \mathbf{subs}\ p \land [x/y]\ \mathbf{subs}\ q\\
&[x/y]\ \mathbf{subs}\ (\lambda d \mid p \bullet q) = \lambda [x/y]\ \mathbf{subs}\ d \mid [x/y]\ \mathbf{subs}\ p \bullet [x/y]\ \mathbf{subs}\ q\\
&\qquad \text{if } x \notin \mathbf{vars}(d)\\
&\qquad = \lambda [x/y]\ \mathbf{subs}\ d \mid p \bullet q \quad \text{if } x \in \mathbf{vars}(d)\\
&[x/y]\ \mathbf{subs}\ (s\ t) = [x/y]\ \mathbf{subs}\ s\ [x/y]\ \mathbf{subs}\ t\\
&[x/y]\ \mathbf{subs}\ \{s_1, \ldots, s_n\} = \{[x/y]\ \mathbf{subs}\ s_1, \ldots, [x/y]\ \mathbf{subs}\ s_n\}\\
&[x/y]\ \mathbf{subs}\ (s.y) = [x/y]\ \mathbf{subs}\ s.y\\
&[x/y]\ \mathbf{subs}\ y = x\\
&[x/y]\ \mathbf{subs}\ z = z \quad \text{where } z \text{ is distinct from } y
\end{aligned}$$

4.2 Global Paragraphs

Name

Class definition

Description

A class definition introduces a class in terms of its states, initial states and operations. The states are defined by a state schema together with local type and constant definitions. An initial state schema and operations define the initial states and permissible state changes respectively. Together they define the reachable states which an object of the class may be in.

A class may be defined in terms of one or more other classes via inheritance — the inherited classes' local definitions, state and initial state schemas and operations are merged with those in the class.

All features of a class which are visible features of its objects are listed in a visibility list.

Syntax

```
Paragraph ::=   ┌─ClassName [FormalParameters] ─────────
                │ [VisibilityList]
                │ [InheritedClass
                │   ⋮
                │  InheritedClass]
                │ [LocalDefinition
                │   ⋮
                │  LocalDefinition]
                │ [State]
                │ [InitialState]
                │ [Operation
                │   ⋮
                │  Operation]
                └────────────────────────────────────────
```

Rules

A class's name must be distinct from the names of all global variables and constants, (global) schemas and other classes in the specification. The formal generic parameters can only be used in expressions in the class body in which any possible type could be used. A type or feature of an inherited class and a type or feature defined explicitly with the same name must be type compatible.

Definition

Consider the following class definition.

$$
\begin{array}{|l}
\hline
A[X_1,\ldots,X_n] \\
VL \\
A_1 \\
\vdots \\
A_m \\
LD_1 \\
\vdots \\
LD_i \\
ST \\
IN \\
Op_1 \mathrel{\widehat=} OP_1 \\
\vdots \\
Op_j \mathrel{\widehat=} OP_j \\
\hline
\end{array}
$$

$$\textbf{visible}(A[X_1,\ldots,X_n]) = \textbf{visible}(VL)$$

$$\textbf{inherited}(A[X_1,\ldots,X_n]) = s \cup \{A_1,\ldots,A_m\}$$
$$\text{where } s = \textbf{inherited}(A_1) \cup \ldots \cup \textbf{inherited}(A_m)$$

$$\textbf{types}(A[X_1,\ldots,X_n]) = s \cup \textbf{types}(LD_1) \cup \ldots \cup \textbf{types}(LD_i)$$
$$\text{where } s = \textbf{types}(A_1) \cup \ldots \cup \textbf{types}(A_m)$$

$$\textbf{state}(A[X_1,\ldots,X_n]) = [\mathit{self} : A[X_1,\ldots,X_n]] \wedge S \bullet T \bullet \textbf{state}(ST)$$
$$\text{where } S = (\textbf{state}(A_1) \setminus (\mathit{self})) \wedge \ldots \wedge (\textbf{state}(A_m) \setminus (\mathit{self}))$$
$$T = \textbf{state}(LD_1) \bullet \ldots \bullet \textbf{state}(LD_i)$$

$$\textbf{init}(A[X_1,\ldots,X_n]) = S \bullet \textbf{init}(IN)$$
$$\text{where } S = \textbf{init}(A_1) \wedge \ldots \wedge \textbf{init}(A_m)$$

$$\mathbf{Op_k}(A[X_1,\ldots,X_n])) = (s \cup t, S \bullet \textbf{schema}(Op_k \mathrel{\widehat=} OP_k))$$
$$\text{where } k \in 1 \mathinner{..} j$$
$$s = \mathit{first}(\mathbf{Op_k}(B_1)) \cup \ldots \cup \mathit{first}(\mathbf{Op_k}(B_l))$$
$$t = \textbf{delta}(Op_k \mathrel{\widehat=} OP_k)$$
$$S = \mathit{second}(\mathbf{Op_k}(B_1)) \wedge \ldots \wedge \mathit{second}(\mathbf{Op_k}(B_l))$$
$$\{A_1,\ldots,A_m\} \cap \operatorname{dom} \mathbf{Op_k} = \{B_1,\ldots,B_l\}$$

$$\begin{array}{l}\mathbf{Op}(A[X_1,\ldots,X_n]) = (s,S)\\ \quad \text{where } \; Op \notin \{Op_1,\ldots,Op_j\}\\ \qquad\qquad s = \mathit{first}(\mathbf{Op_k}(B_1)) \cup \ldots \cup \mathit{first}(\mathbf{Op_k}(B_l))\\ \qquad\qquad S = \mathit{second}(\mathbf{Op_k}(B_1)) \wedge \ldots \wedge \mathit{second}(\mathbf{Op_k}(B_l))\\ \qquad\qquad \{A_1,\ldots,A_m\} \cap \operatorname{dom} \mathbf{Op} = \{B_1,\ldots,B_l\} \neq \varnothing\end{array}$$

4.3 Class Paragraphs

Name

Visibility list

Description

The visibility list defines the interface of a class — that is, those features of objects of the class which are visible. When no visibility list is given in a class, all features are visible.

Syntax

$$\mathsf{VisibilityList} ::= \upharpoonright(\mathsf{Identifier},\ldots,\mathsf{Identifier})$$

Rules

Each name in the visibility list of a class must be the name of a feature — possibly an inherited feature — of the class.

Definition

$$\textbf{visible}(\upharpoonright(x_1,\ldots,x_n,\mathit{INIT},Op_1,\ldots,Op_m)) = \{x_1,\ldots,x_n,\mathit{INIT},Op_1,\ldots,Op_m\}$$

Name

Inherited class

Description

An inherited class designator is used to specify a class being inherited by another class. The inherited class must have any generic parameters instantiated by actual parameters and may have one or more features renamed.

Syntax

InheritedClass ::= ClassName *[*ActualParameters*]* *[*RenameList*]*

Rules

An inherited class's name must be that of a class defined previously in the specification. A class cannot inherit itself. The number of actual parameters must match the number of generic parameters in the class definition. The "old" names in the rename list must be of attributes or operations of the defined class, or of auxiliary variables of its operations. The "old" names must also be distinct. If a "new" name appears twice in a rename list then the features corresponding to the associated "old" names must be type compatible. If a "new" name is the same as that of an existing feature of the class then that feature and the feature corresponding to the associated "old" name must be type compatible.

Definition

Let class $A[X_1, \ldots, X_n]$ have operations $Op_1, \ldots, Op_i$ and consider the following inherited class designator B.

$$B = A[t_1, \ldots, t_n][x_1/y_1, \ldots, x_m/y_m, Op_{i+1}/Op_1, \ldots, Op_{i+j}/Op_j]$$
where $j \leq i$

$$\mathbf{types}(B) = \mathbf{types}(A[X_1, \ldots, X_n])$$

$$\mathbf{inherited}(B) = \mathbf{inherited}(A[X_1, \ldots, X_n])$$

$$\mathbf{state}(B) = [t_1/X_1, \ldots, t_n/X_n] \ \mathbf{subs\ state}(A[X_1, \ldots, X_n])[x_1/y_1, \ldots, x_m/y_m]$$

$$\mathbf{init}(B) = [t_1/X_1, \ldots, t_n/X_n] \ \mathbf{subs\ init}(A[X_1, \ldots, X_n])[x_1/y_1, \ldots, x_m/y_m]$$

$$\mathbf{Op_{i+k}}(B) = [t_1/X_1, \ldots, t_n/X_n, x_1/y_1, \ldots, x_m/y_m] \ \mathbf{subs\ Op_k}(A[X_1, \ldots, X_n])$$
where $k \in 1 \mathinner{..} j$

$$\mathbf{Op_k}(B) = [t_1/X_1, \ldots, t_n/X_n, x_1/y_1, \ldots, x_m/y_m] \ \mathbf{subs\ Op_k}(A[X_1, \ldots, X_n])$$
where $k \in j+1 \mathinner{..} i$

Name

Basic type

Description

A local basic type definition introduces one or more basic types which are local to the class.

Syntax

$$\text{LocalDefinition} ::= [\text{Identifier}, \ldots, \text{Identifier}]$$

Rules

The names of the basic types must be distinct from any names occurring before them in the class.

Definition

$$\textbf{types}([t_1, \ldots, t_n]) = \{t_1, \ldots, t_n\}$$

$$\textbf{state}([t_1, \ldots, t_n]) = [\text{true}]$$

Name

Axiomatic definition

Description

A local axiomatic definition introduces one or more constants which are local to the class.

Syntax

$$\text{LocalDefinition} ::= \llbracket \; \begin{array}{|l} \text{Declaration} \\ \hline \text{PredicateList} \end{array} \rrbracket$$

Rules

The names of the constants must be distinct from any names occurring before them in the class.

Definition

$$\mathbf{types}(d \mid p) = \varnothing$$

$$\mathbf{state}(d \mid p) = [\, d \mid p \,]$$

Name

Abbreviation definition

Description

A local abbreviation definition introduces a type which is local to the class.

Syntax

LocalDefinition ::= Identifier == Expression

Rules

The name of the type must be distinct from any name occurring before it in the class.

Definition

$$\textbf{types}(t == s) = \{t\}$$

$$\textbf{state}(t == s) = \left[\, t = s \,\right]$$

Name

Free type

Description

A local free type definition introduces a free type which is local to the class.

Syntax

$$\mathsf{LocalDefinition} ::= \mathsf{Identifier} ::= \mathsf{Branch} \mid \ldots \mid \mathsf{Branch}$$

Rules

The name of the type must be distinct from any name occurring before it in the class. The identifiers in the branches of the definition must be distinct from the name of the type, each other, and all names occurring before the definition in the class.

Definition

A local free type definition introduces, as well as a type, a constant for each branch. These constants represent the complete set of values of the type as detailed in J.M. Spivey's *The Z Notation* (Prentice Hall, 1989 & 1992).

$$\textbf{types}(t ::= x_1 \mid \ldots \mid x_n \mid y_1 \langle\langle s_1[t] \rangle\rangle \mid \ldots \mid y_m \langle\langle s_m[t] \rangle\rangle) = \{t\}$$

$$\textbf{state}(t ::= x_1 \mid \ldots \mid x_n \mid y_1 \langle\langle s_1[t] \rangle\rangle \mid \ldots \mid y_m \langle\langle s_m[t] \rangle\rangle) =$$

$$\begin{array}{|l}
x_1, \ldots, x_n : t \\
y_1 : s_1[t] \rightarrowtail t; \ \ldots; \ y_m : s_m[t] \rightarrowtail t \\
\hline
\text{disjoint}\langle \{x_1\}, \ldots, \{x_n\}, \text{ran}\, y_1, \ldots, \text{ran}\, y_m \rangle \\
\forall z : \mathbb{P}\, t \bullet \\
\quad \{x_1, \ldots, x_n\} \cup y_1 (\!|\, s_1[z] \,|\!) \cup \ldots \cup y_m (\!|\, s_m[t] \,|\!) \subseteq z \Rightarrow t \subseteq z
\end{array}$$

Name

State schema

Description

The state schema defines the state variables of the class. Together with the local axiomatic definitions, it defines the states of the class. The state variables are partitioned into primary and secondary variables — the latter may be implicitly changed by any operation and are generally used to conveniently access otherwise derivable information.

Syntax

$$\begin{aligned}\mathsf{State} ::= &\ [\,\mathsf{Declaration}\ [\Delta\ \mathsf{Declaration}]\ [\ |\ \mathsf{Predicate}]\,]\\ |\ &\ [\,\Delta\ \mathsf{Declaration}\ [\ |\ \mathsf{Predicate}]\,]\\ |\ &\ [\,\mathsf{Predicate}\,]\end{aligned}$$

Rules

The names of the state variables must be distinct from any names occurring before them in the class.

Definition

$$\mathbf{state}([\, d_1 \Delta d_2 \mid p \,]) = [\, d_1;\ d_2 \mid p \,]$$

$$\mathbf{secondary}([\, d_1 \Delta x_1 : t_1;\ \ldots;\ x_n : t_n \mid p \,]) = \{x_1, \ldots, x_n\}$$

Name

Initial state schema

Description

The initial state schema of a class defines the initial states of a class — that is, the states its objects are in before they undergo any operations. It has no declarations but may refer to the implicitly available state variables of the class.

Syntax

$$\mathsf{InitialState} ::= \mathit{INIT} \mathrel{\widehat{=}} [\mathsf{Predicate}]$$

Definition

An initial state schema in class A is defined as follows.

$$\mathbf{init}(\mathit{INIT} \mathrel{\widehat{=}} [p]) = [\mathbf{state}(A) \mid p]$$

Name

Operation

Description

An operation defines one or more permissible changes of state that an object of its class may undergo. Together with the initial state schema, the operations define the reachable states of the class — that is, the states of the class that an object of the class may be in.

An operation's declarations and predicates may refer to the implicitly available pre- and post-values of state variables of the class.

Syntax

$$\mathsf{Operation} ::= \mathsf{OperationName} \mathrel{\widehat=} \mathsf{OperationExpression}$$

Rules

An operation's name must be distinct from any name occurring before it in the class.

Definition

An operation in class A is defined as follows.

$$\mathbf{delta}(Op \mathrel{\widehat=} OP) = \mathbf{delta}(OP)$$

$$\mathbf{schema}(Op \mathrel{\widehat=} OP) = \Delta\mathbf{state}(A) \bullet \mathbf{schema}(OP)$$

Note

The meaning of ΔS in Object-Z differs from that in Z — it is not simply $S \wedge S'$. Given that a is an object identity declared in S, expressions of the form $a.x$ in S are replaced by $a'.x$ in S'. However, $a'.x$ refers to the pre-state value of the x variable of a', not its post-state value.

Object-Z does not have a notation to refer to the post-state value of a variable of an object identified by a variable such as a'. Hence, it is generally not possible to expand ΔS in terms of declarations and predicates. For the purposes of the definitions in this chapter, however, we will let this value be denoted by $a'.x'$ so that ΔS can be expanded as in the following example.

Given $S = [\, a : A \mid a.x < 10 \,]$, $\Delta S = [\, a, a' : A \mid a.x < 10 \wedge a'.x' < 10 \,]$.

4.4 Operation Expressions

Name

Operation schema

Description

An operation schema is used to specify an operation of a class in terms of its attributes and a set of declared auxiliary variables. Any primary variables which the operation may change are included in its Δ-list.

Syntax

$$\begin{aligned} \mathsf{OperationExpression} ::= &\ \big[\, \mathsf{DeltaList}\ \mathit{/}\mathsf{Declaration}\mathit{/}\ \mathit{/}\mid \mathsf{Predicate}\mathit{/}\,\big] \\ \mid &\ \big[\, \mathsf{Declaration}\ \mathit{/}\mid \mathsf{Predicate}\mathit{/}\,\big] \\ \mid &\ \big[\, \mathit{/}\mathsf{Predicate}\mathit{/}\,\big] \end{aligned}$$

Rules

The Δ-list may only include primary variables of the class. The names of auxiliary variables must be distinct from any feature names occurring before the operation schema in the class.

Definition

$$\mathbf{delta}(\big[\Delta(x_1,\ldots,x_n)\ d \mid p\big]) = \{x_1,\ldots,x_n\}$$

$$\mathbf{schema}(\big[\Delta(x_1,\ldots,x_n)\ d \mid p\big]) = \big[\, d \mid p\,\big]$$

Name

Operation promotion

Description

Operation promotion is used to specify that an identified object undergoes a particular operation. The resulting operation has an empty Δ-list because it doesn't change any of the variables of the class in which it occurs — although the object is changed, the identity itself is not. Its auxiliary variables are those of the operation applied to the object.

Syntax

OperationExpression ::= Expression.Identifier [RenameList]

Rules

The expression must evaluate to an object identity and the identifier must be the name of a visible operation in the class of the identified object. The form of the optional rename list is as for operation identifiers (page 93). In the case where the type of the object identity is a polymorphic type or a class union and is not further qualified, the operation must be visible in all classes of the type.

Definition

Let $a \in A$ and Op be the name of a visible operation in A such that $second(\mathbf{Op}(A)) = [d \mid p]$.

The definition requires the introduction of the notation $a.t$ to represent a type t defined in A. Also, as discussed on page 89, we use $a.x'$ to denote the post-state value of $a.x$.

$$\mathbf{delta}(a.Op[y_{j+1}/y_1, \ldots, y_{2*j}/y_j]) = \varnothing$$

$$\begin{aligned}
&\mathbf{schema}(a.Op[y_{j+1}/y_1, \ldots, y_{2*j}/y_j]) = \\
&\qquad\qquad [\, S \mid a.x_1' = a.x_1 \land \ldots \land a.x_i' = a.x_i \,][y_{j+1}/y_1, \ldots, y_{2*j}/y_j] \\
&\text{ where } \mathbf{types}(A) = \{t_1, \ldots, t_n\} \\
&\qquad \mathbf{vars}(\Delta\mathbf{state}(A)) = \{x_1, \ldots, x_m\} \\
&\qquad \mathbf{vars}(\mathbf{state}(A)) \setminus (\mathit{first}(\mathbf{Op}(A)) \cup \mathbf{secondary}(A)) = \{x_1, \ldots, x_i\} \\
&\qquad T = [\, d \,] \setminus (x_1, \ldots, x_m) \\
&\qquad S = [a.t_1/t_1, \ldots, a.t_n/t_n, a.x_1/x_1, \ldots, a.x_m/x_m] \\
&\qquad\qquad \mathbf{subs}\ [\, T \mid p \,]
\end{aligned}$$

Illustrative example

As an example of the definition of operation promotion, consider defining the schema part of $a.Op[in?/x?]$ where a identifies an object of the following class.

A

$[t]$

$x, y : t$

Op

$\Delta(x)$

$x? : t$

$x' = x?$

$$\mathit{second}(\mathbf{Op}(A)) = [x, x', y, y', x? : t \mid x' = x?]$$
$$\mathbf{types}(A) = \{t\}$$
$$\mathbf{vars}(\Delta\mathbf{state}(A)) = \{x, y, x', y'\}$$
$$\mathbf{vars}(\mathbf{state}(A)) \setminus (\mathit{first}(\mathbf{Op}(A)) \cup \mathbf{secondary}(A)) = \{y\}$$

Therefore,

$$\begin{aligned} T &= [x, x', y, y', x? : t] \setminus (x, x', y, y') \\ &= [x? : t] \end{aligned}$$

and

$$\begin{aligned} S &= [a.t/t, a.x/x, a.y/y, a.x'/x', a.y'/y'] \ \mathbf{subs} \ [T \mid x' = x?] \\ &= [x? : a.t \mid a.x' = x?]. \end{aligned}$$

Therefore,

$$\begin{aligned} \mathbf{schema}(a.Op[in?/x?]) &= [S \mid a.y' = a.y][in?/x?] \\ &= [in? : a.t \mid a.x' = in? \land a.y' = a.y] \end{aligned}$$

Name

Operation identifier

Description

An operation may be defined in terms of another operation with its auxiliary variables possibly renamed.

Syntax

OperationExpression ::= Identifier [RenameList]

Rules

The identifier must be the name of a previously defined operation of the class, or the operation being defined. The "old" names in the rename list must be of auxiliary variables of the operation. The "old" names must also be distinct. If a "new" name appears twice in a rename list then the auxiliary variables corresponding to the associated "old" names must be type compatible. If a "new" name is the same as that of an existing auxiliary variable of the operation then that auxiliary variable and the auxiliary variable corresponding to the associated "old" name must be type compatible.

Definition

An operation identifier in class A is defined as follows.

$$\mathbf{delta}(Op[x_1/y_1,\ldots,x_n/y_n]) = \mathit{first}(\mathbf{Op}(A))$$

$$\mathbf{schema}(Op[x_1/y_1,\ldots,x_n/y_n]) = \mathit{second}(\mathbf{Op}(A))[x_1/y_1,\ldots,x_n/y_n]$$

Name

Conjunction

Description

The conjunction operator is a binary operator which can be used to specify simultaneous occurrence of operations. It is commutative and associative.

Syntax

$$\mathsf{OperationExpression} ::= \mathsf{OperationExpression} \wedge \mathsf{OperationExpression}$$

Rules

Common-named variables declared in the arguments must be type compatible.

Definition

$$\mathbf{delta}(OP_1 \wedge OP_2) = \mathbf{delta}(OP_1) \cup \mathbf{delta}(OP_2)$$

$$\mathbf{schema}(OP_1 \wedge OP_2) = \mathbf{schema}(OP_1) \wedge \mathbf{schema}(OP_2)$$

Name

Parallel composition

Description

The parallel composition operator is a binary operator which may be used to specify inter-object communication. The operator identifies and equates input variables in either argument with output variables in the other having the same basename, i.e. apart from the ? or !. The identified input and output variables are hidden in the resulting operation. The operator is commutative but not associative.

Syntax

$$\mathsf{OperationExpression} ::= \mathsf{OperationExpression} \parallel \mathsf{OperationExpression}$$

Rules

Common-named variables declared in the arguments must be type compatible. Inputs and outputs with common basenames declared in different arguments must be type compatible. Inputs and outputs with common basenames declared in the same argument must be type compatible when an output parameter with the same basename is declared in the other argument.

Definition

Provided $z_1, \ldots, z_{n+m}$ do not appear as free variables in OP_1 and OP_2, parallel composition is defined as follows.

$$\mathbf{delta}(OP_1 \parallel OP_2) = \mathbf{delta}(OP_1) \cup \mathbf{delta}(OP_2)$$

$$\begin{aligned}
&\mathbf{schema}(OP_1 \parallel OP_2) = \\
&\qquad (\mathbf{schema}(OP_1)[z_1/x_1?, \ldots, z_n/x_n?, z_{n+1}/y_1!, \ldots, z_{n+m}/y_m!] \\
&\qquad \wedge \\
&\qquad \mathbf{schema}(OP_2)[z_1/x_1!, \ldots, z_n/x_n!, z_{n+1}/y_1?, \ldots, z_{n+m}/y_m?]) \\
&\qquad \setminus (z_1, \ldots, z_{n+m}) \\
&\text{where } \mathbf{inputs}(OP_1) \cap \mathbf{outputs}(OP_2) = \{x_1, \ldots, x_n\} \\
&\qquad \mathbf{inputs}(OP_2) \cap \mathbf{outputs}(OP_1) = \{y_1, \ldots, y_m\}
\end{aligned}$$

Name

Associative parallel composition

Description

The associative parallel composition operator is a binary operator which can be used to specify inter-object communication. The operator identifies and equates input variables in either argument with output variables in the other having the same basename, i.e. apart from the ? or !. The identified input variables are hidden in the resulting operation; the output variables are not hidden and so may be equated with other input variables in subsequent parallel compositions. The operator is commutative and associative.

Syntax

$$\mathsf{OperationExpression} ::= \mathsf{OperationExpression} \parallel_{!} \mathsf{OperationExpression}$$

Rules

Common-named variables declared in the arguments must be type compatible. Inputs and outputs with common basenames declared in different arguments must be type compatible. Inputs and outputs with common basenames declared in the same argument must be type compatible when an output parameter with the same basename is declared in the other argument.

Definition

$$\mathbf{delta}(OP_1 \parallel_{!} OP_2) = \mathbf{delta}(OP_1) \cup \mathbf{delta}(OP_2)$$

$$\begin{aligned} \mathbf{schema}(OP_1 \parallel_{!} OP_2) = {} & \mathbf{schema}(OP_1)[x_1!/x_1?, \ldots, x_n!/x_n?] \\ & \wedge \\ & \mathbf{schema}(OP_2)[y_1!/y_1?, \ldots, y_m!/y_m?] \end{aligned}$$
$$\text{where } \mathbf{inputs}(OP_1) \cap \mathbf{outputs}(OP_2) = \{x_1, \ldots, x_n\}$$
$$\mathbf{inputs}(OP_2) \cap \mathbf{outputs}(OP_1) = \{y_1, \ldots, y_m\}$$

Name

Nondeterministic choice

Description

The nondeterministic choice operator is a binary operator which is used to specify angelic choice between operations. It may also be used to specify internal — that is, non-environmentally controlled — choice between enabled operations. It is associative and commutative.

Syntax

OperationExpression ::= OperationExpression [] OperationExpression

Rules

The declared variable names in each argument must be the same and common-named variables must be type compatible.

Definition

$$\mathbf{delta}(OP_1 \mathbin{[]} OP_2) = \mathbf{delta}(OP_1) \cup \mathbf{delta}(OP_2)$$

$$\begin{aligned}\mathbf{schema}(OP_1 \mathbin{[]} OP_2) = {} & [\mathbf{schema}(OP_1) \mid x_1' = x_1 \wedge \ldots \wedge x_n' = x_n] \\ & \vee \\ & [\mathbf{schema}(OP_2) \mid y_1' = y_1 \wedge \ldots \wedge y_m' = y_m]\end{aligned}$$

$$\begin{aligned}\text{where }\ & \mathbf{delta}(OP_2) \setminus \mathbf{delta}(OP_1) = \{x_1, \ldots, x_n\} \\ & \mathbf{delta}(OP_1) \setminus \mathbf{delta}(OP_2) = \{y_1, \ldots, y_m\}\end{aligned}$$

Name

Sequential composition

Description

The sequential composition operator is a binary operator used to model two operations occurring in sequence. The resulting atomic operation is only enabled when the first operation in the sequence can occur and result in a state from which the second operation can occur. The operations also communicate — the output variables of the first operation in the sequence are equated with those in the second operation having the same basename — that is, apart from the ? and !. Such equated input and output variables are hidden in the resulting operation. The operator is neither commutative nor associative.

Syntax

$$\mathsf{OperationExpression} ::= \mathsf{OperationExpression} \mathbin{\S} \mathsf{OperationExpression}$$

Rules

Undecorated variables in the first argument and primed variables in the second argument with the same basenames must be compatible. Inputs declared in the first argument and outputs in the second with the same basenames must be type compatible. Common-named variables declared in both arguments which do not fall into one of the categories above must be type compatible.

Definition

The definition of sequential composition is complicated by the possibility of object aliasing. An intermediate state — between the two operation occurrences — needs to be defined such that any aliasing is taken into account. Here we present a partial definition in which the argument operations OP_1 and OP_2 are such that $\mathbf{schema}(OP_1) = [\, d_1 \mid p_1 \,]$ and $\mathbf{schema}(OP_2) = [\, d_2 \mid p_2 \,]$ and there does not exist a bound object identity — occurring in the declaration of an existential or universal quantifier, for example — in p_1 or p_2.

In the following, we utilize the notation for post-state values of identified objects described on page 89 and allow object identities of possibly different classes to be compared as discussed on page 109.

The values of the primed attributes of all objects referenced by OP_1 — that is, values denoted by expressions of the form $a.x'$ — form part of the intermediate state of the sequential composition. Similarly, the values of the unprimed attributes of all objects referenced by OP_2 — that is, values denoted by expressions of the form $a.x$ — form part of the intermediate state of the sequential composition. Expressions denoting these values must not appear in the predicate of the resulting operation expression. Furthermore, expressions of the form $a'.x'$ in OP_1 must be equated with $a.x$ in OP_2 provided a is a variable of OP_2, and expressions of the form $a!.x'$ in OP_1 must be equated with $a?.x$ in OP_2 provided $a?$ is a variable of OP_2.

Let the expressions $a_1.x_1', \ldots, a_n.x_n'$ denote all the primed attributes of all the objects referenced by OP_1, and let $a_1.x_1 \in t_1, \ldots, a_n.x_n \in t_n$. Similarly, let the expressions $a_{n+1}.x_{n+1}, \ldots, a_{n+m}.x_{n+m}$ denote all the unprimed attributes of all the objects referenced by OP_2, and let $a_{n+1}.x_{n+1} \in t_{n+1}, \ldots, a_{n+m}.x_{n+m} \in t_{n+m}$.

Sequential composition in class A is defined in terms of Z sequential composition as follows.
1. Replace $a_1.x_1', \ldots, a_n.x_n'$ in p_1 with variables $z_1, \ldots, z_n$ which do not occur free in OP_1 or OP_2.

$$[\![p_3]\!] = [\![[z_1/a_1.x_1', \ldots, z_n/a_n.x_n'] \textbf{ subs } p_1]\!]$$

2. Replace $a_{n+1}.x_{n+1}, \ldots, a_{n+m}.x_{n+m}$ in p_2 with variables $z_{n+1}, \ldots, z_{n+m}$ which do not occur free in OP_1, in primed or unprimed form, or in OP_2.

$$[\![p_4]\!] = [\![[z_{n+1}/a_{n+1}.x_{n+1}, \ldots, z_{n+m}/a_{n+m}.x_{n+m}] \textbf{ subs } p_2]\!]$$

3. For each $a_i.x_i$ $(i \in 1 \mathinner{..} n)$ such that a_i is primed or an output variable, add a predicate to OP_1 of the form $a_i = a_j \Rightarrow z_i = z_j$ for all $j \in 1 \mathinner{..} n$. Let the conjunction of all such predicates be denoted p_5.
4. For each $a_i.x_i$ $(i \in n+1 \mathinner{..} n+m)$ such that a_i is undecorated or an input variable, add a predicate to OP_2 of the form $a_i = a_j \Rightarrow z_i = z_j$ for all $j \in n+1 \mathinner{..} n+m$. Let the conjunction of all such predicates be denoted p_6.
5. For each $a_i.x_i$ $(i \in 1 \mathinner{..} n)$ and $a_j.x_j$ $(j \in n+1 \mathinner{..} n+m)$ such that a_i is undecorated and a_j is primed, or a_i is an output and a_j is an input, and a_i and a_j have the same basenames, add a predicate to OP_2 equating z_i and z_j. Let the conjunction of all such predicates be denoted p_7.

Provided $y_1, \ldots, y_k$ do not occur free in OP_1, in primed or unprimed form, or in OP_2, sequential composition is defined as follows.

$$\textbf{delta}(OP_1 \fatsemi OP_2) = \textbf{delta}(OP_1) \cup \textbf{delta}(OP_2)$$

$$\begin{array}{l}\textbf{schema}(OP_1 \fatsemi OP_2) = \\ \quad ([\, d_1;\ z_1 : t_1, \ldots, z_n : t_n \mid p_3 \wedge p_5 \wedge y_{k+1}' = y_{k+1} \wedge \ldots \wedge y_{k+l}' = y_{k+l}\,] \\ \quad [y_1/y_1!, \ldots, y_k/y_k!] \\ \quad \fatsemi \\ \quad [\, d_2;\ z_1 : t_1, \ldots, z_{n+m} : t_{n+m} \mid p_4 \wedge p_6 \wedge p_7\,][y_1/y_1?, \ldots, y_k/y_k?]) \\ \quad \backslash (z_1, \ldots, z_{n+m}, y_1, \ldots, y_k) \\ \text{where } \textbf{outputs}(OP_1) \cap \textbf{inputs}(OP_2) = \{y_1, \ldots, y_k\} \\ \qquad \textbf{vars}(\textbf{state}(A)) \setminus (\textbf{delta}(OP_1) \cup \textbf{secondary}(A)) = \{y_{k+1}, \ldots, y_{k+l}\}\end{array}$$

Illustrative example

As an example of the definition of sequential composition, consider the following classes.

B

$x : \mathbb{N}$

Op

$\Delta(x)$
$y?, y! : \mathbb{N}$

$x' = x + y?$
$y! = y?$

A

$a, b : B$

$Op \mathrel{\widehat=} a.Op \mathbin{\fatsemi} b.Op$

$$
\begin{aligned}
&\textbf{schema}(a.Op) = [\, y?, y! : \mathbb{N} \mid a.x' = a.x + y? \land y! = y? \,] \\
&\textbf{schema}(b.Op) = [\, y?, y! : \mathbb{N} \mid b.x' = b.x + y? \land y! = y? \,] \\
&\textbf{vars}(\textbf{state}(A)) \setminus (\textbf{delta}(a.Op) \cup \textbf{secondary}(A)) = \{a, b\} \\
&\textbf{outputs}(a.Op) \cap \textbf{inputs}(b.Op) = \{y\}
\end{aligned}
$$

Therefore,

$$
\begin{aligned}
[\, p_3 \,] &= [\, [z_1/a.x', z_2/b.x', z_3/a'.x', z_4/b'.x'] \; \textbf{subs} \; (a.x' = a.x + y? \land y! = y?) \,] \\
&= [\, z_1 = a.x + y? \land y! = y? \,]
\end{aligned}
$$

$$
\begin{aligned}
[\, p_4 \,] &= [\, [z_5/a.x, z_6/b.x, z_7/a'.x, z_8/b'.x] \; \textbf{subs} \; (b.x' = b.x + y? \land y! = y?) \,] \\
&= [\, b.x' = z_6 + y? \land y? = y! \,]
\end{aligned}
$$

$$
\begin{aligned}
[\, p_5 \,] = [\, &(a' = a \Rightarrow z_3 = z_1) \land (a' = b \Rightarrow z_3 = z_2) \land (a' = b' \Rightarrow z_3 = z_4) \land \\
&(b' = a \Rightarrow z_4 = z_1) \land (b' = b \Rightarrow z_4 = z_2) \,]
\end{aligned}
$$

$$
\begin{aligned}
[\, p_6 \,] = [\, &(a = b \Rightarrow z_5 = z_6) \land (a = a' \Rightarrow z_5 = z_7) \land (a = b' \Rightarrow z_5 = z_8) \land \\
&(b = a' \Rightarrow z_6 = z_7) \land (b = b' \Rightarrow z_6 = z_8) \,]
\end{aligned}
$$

$$
[\, p_7 \,] = [\, z_3 = z_5 \land z_4 = z_6 \,]
$$

Therefore,

$$\begin{aligned}
&\textbf{schema}(a.Op \fatsemi b.Op)\\
&= ([\, y?, y!, z_1, z_2, z_3, z_4 : \mathbb{N} \mid z_1 = a.x + y? \land y! = y? \land\\
&\qquad (a' = a \Rightarrow z_3 = z_1) \land (a' = b \Rightarrow z_3 = z_2) \land (a' = b' \Rightarrow z_3 = z_4) \land\\
&\qquad (b' = a \Rightarrow z_4 = z_1) \land (b' = b \Rightarrow z_4 = z_2) \land\\
&\qquad a' = a \land b' = b \,][y/y!]\\
&\quad \fatsemi\\
&\quad [\, y?, y!, z_1, z_2, z_3, z_4, z_5, z_6, z_7, z_8 : \mathbb{N} \mid b.x' = z_6 + y? \land y! = y? \land\\
&\qquad (a = b \Rightarrow z_5 = z_6) \land (a = a' \Rightarrow z_5 = z_7) \land (a = b' \Rightarrow z_5 = z_8) \land\\
&\qquad (b = a' \Rightarrow z_6 = z_7) \land (b = b' \Rightarrow z_6 = z_8) \land\\
&\qquad z_3 = z_5 \land z_4 = z_6 \,][y/y?])\\
&\quad \setminus (z_1, z_2, z_3, z_4, z_5, z_6, z_7, z_8, y)
\end{aligned}$$

$$\begin{aligned}
&= ([\, y?, y!, z_1, z_2, z_3, z_4 : \mathbb{N} \mid z_1 = a.x + y? \land y! = y? \land\\
&\qquad z_3 = z_1 \land (a = b \Rightarrow z_3 = z_2 = z_4 = z_1) \land z_4 = z_2 \land\\
&\qquad a' = a \land b' = b \,][y'/y!]\\
&\quad \fatsemi\\
&\quad [\, y?, y!, z_1, z_2, z_3, z_4, z_5, z_6, z_7, z_8 : \mathbb{N} \mid b.x' = z_6 + y? \land y! = y? \land\\
&\qquad (a = b \Rightarrow z_5 = z_6) \land (a = a' \Rightarrow z_5 = z_7) \land (a = b' \Rightarrow z_5 = z_8) \land\\
&\qquad (b = a' \Rightarrow z_6 = z_7) \land (b = b' \Rightarrow z_6 = z_8) \land\\
&\qquad z_3 = z_5 \land z_4 = z_6 \,][y/y?])\\
&\quad \setminus (z_1, z_2, z_3, z_4, z_5, z_6, z_7, z_8, y)
\end{aligned}$$

$$\begin{aligned}
&= [\, y?, y! : \mathbb{N} \mid \exists : z_1, z_2, z_3, z_4, z_5, z_6, z_7, z_8, y : \mathbb{N};\ a_0, b_0 : B \bullet\\
&\qquad z_1 = a.x + y? \land y = y? \land a_0 = a \land b_0 = b \land\\
&\qquad b_0.x' = z_6 + y? \land y = y! \land\\
&\qquad z_1 = z_3 \land z_4 = z_2 \land z_3 = z_5 \land z_4 = z_6 \land\\
&\qquad (a_0 = b_0 \Rightarrow z_3 = z_2 = z_4 = z_1) \land (a_0 = b_0 \Rightarrow z_5 = z_6) \land\\
&\qquad (a_0 = a' \Rightarrow z_5 = z_7) \land (a_0 = b' \Rightarrow z_5 = z_8) \land\\
&\qquad (b_0 = a' \Rightarrow z_6 = z_7) \land (b_0 = b' \Rightarrow z_6 = z_8) \,]
\end{aligned}$$

$$= [\, y?, y! : \mathbb{N} \mid b.x' \geqslant y? \land y! = y? \land (a = b \Rightarrow b.x' = a.x + y? + y?) \,]$$

Name

Scope enrichment

Description

The scope enrichment operator is a binary operator which enables the scope of the declarations in one operation to extend to the declarations and predicates of another.

Syntax

OperationExpression ::= OperationExpression • OperationExpression

Rules

Common-named variables declared in the arguments must be type compatible.

Definition

$$\mathbf{delta}(OP_1 \bullet OP_2) = \mathbf{delta}(OP_1) \cup \mathbf{delta}(OP_2)$$

$$\mathbf{schema}(OP_1 \bullet OP_2) = [\mathbf{schema}(OP_1);\ d \mid p]$$
where $\mathbf{schema}(OP_1) \Rightarrow (\mathbf{schema}(OP_2) \Leftrightarrow [d \mid p])$
for all $v \in \mathbf{vars}(\mathbf{schema}(OP_1))$, v does not occur free in d

Illustrative example

Let $OP_1 \mathrel{\widehat=} [y : \mathbb{P}\,\mathbb{N}]$ and $OP_2 \mathrel{\widehat=} [x : y]$.

$$\mathbf{schema}(OP_1) \Leftrightarrow y \in \mathbb{P}\,\mathbb{N}$$
$$\mathbf{schema}(OP_2) \Leftrightarrow x \in y$$

Since

$$\mathbf{schema}(OP_1) \Rightarrow (\mathbf{schema}(OP_2) \Leftrightarrow [x : \mathbb{N} \mid x \in y])$$

and

$$\mathbf{vars}(\mathbf{schema}(OP_1)) = \{y\} \text{ and } y \text{ does not occur free in } x : \mathbb{N},$$

$$OP_1 \bullet OP_2 = [y : \mathbb{P}\,\mathbb{N};\ x : \mathbb{N} \mid x \in y].$$

Name

Hiding

Description

The hiding operator is used to hide auxiliary variables of an operation.

Syntax

$$\mathsf{OperationExpression} ::= \mathsf{OperationExpression} \backslash (\mathsf{Identifier}, \ldots, \mathsf{Identifier})$$

Rules

The variables to be hidden must be auxiliary variables of the operation.

Definition

$$\mathbf{delta}(OP \setminus (x_1, \ldots, x_n)) = \mathbf{delta}(OP)$$

$$\mathbf{schema}(OP \setminus (x_1, \ldots, x_n)) = \mathbf{schema}(OP) \setminus (x_1, \ldots, x_n)$$

Name

Distributed conjunction

Description

The distributed conjunction operator is used to conjoin a (possibly infinite) set of operations.

Syntax

OperationExpression ::= $\bigwedge$ Declaration [| Predicate] • OperationExpression

Rules

The variables in the declaration following the distributed operator must be distinct from the auxiliary variables in the operation expression.

Definition

$$\mathbf{delta}(\bigwedge\ d \mid p \bullet OP) = \mathbf{delta}(OP)$$

$$\mathbf{schema}(\bigwedge\ d \mid p \bullet OP) = \forall\, d \mid p \bullet \mathbf{schema}(OP)$$

Name

Distributed nondeterministic choice

Description

The distributed nondeterministic choice operator is used to specify nondeterministic choice between a (possibly infinite) set of operations.

Syntax

OperationExpression ::= $\bigsqcap$ Declaration *[* | Predicate*]* • OperationExpression

Rules

The variables in the declaration following the distributed operator must be distinct from the auxiliary variables in the operation expression.

Definition

Since the Δ-lists of the operations in the set over which the choice is made are identical, the choice is equivalent to standard disjunction (see page 97).

$$\textbf{delta}(\bigsqcap\ d \mid p \bullet OP) = \textbf{delta}(OP)$$

$$\textbf{schema}(\bigsqcap\ d \mid p \bullet OP) = \exists\, d \mid p \bullet \textbf{schema}(OP)$$

Name

Distributed sequential composition

Description

The distributed sequential composition operator is used to sequentially combine a (finite) set of operations.

Syntax

OperationExpression ::= $\fatsemi$ Declaration [| Predicate] • OperationExpression

Rules

The variables in the declaration following the distributed operator must be distinct from the auxiliary variables in the operation expression. Any primed variables in the declaration must have distinct basenames from the undecorated auxiliary variables of the operation expression.

Definition

$$\mathbf{delta}(\fatsemi\, d \mid p \bullet OP) = \mathbf{delta}(OP)$$

$$\begin{array}{ll} \multicolumn{2}{l}{\mathbf{schema}(\fatsemi\, d \mid p \bullet OP) =} \\ & \mathbf{schema}([\, OP;\ d \mid p_1 \,] \fatsemi \ldots \fatsemi [\, OP;\ d \mid p_n \,]) \setminus (x_1, \ldots, x_m) \\ \text{where} & [\, d \mid p \,] = \{s_1, \ldots, s_n\} \\ & [\, d \mid p_1 \,] = \{s_1\} \\ & \vdots \\ & [\, d \mid p_n \,] = \{s_n\} \\ & \mathbf{vars}(d) = \{x_1, \ldots, x_m\} \end{array}$$

4.5 Predicates

Name

Boolean-valued expressions

Description

A Boolean-valued expression evaluates to a logical value — that is, either true or false. Therefore, it can be used as a predicate.

Syntax

Predicate ::= Expression

Definition

The set $\mathbb{B}$ contains exactly two values — one corresponding to true and one to false.

$$
\begin{aligned}
&\forall x, y, z : \mathbb{B} \mid x \land \neg\, y \bullet \\
&\qquad x \neq y \land \\
&\qquad z \Leftrightarrow z = x \land \\
&\qquad \neg\, z \Leftrightarrow z = y
\end{aligned}
$$

Name

Promoted initial state predicates

Description

Initial state predicate promotion is used to specify that an identified object is in its initial state.

Syntax

Predicate ::= Expression.INIT

Rules

The first argument must be an object identity and the class of the identified object must have INIT in its visibility list. In the case where the type of the object identity is a polymorphic type or a class union and is not further qualified, INIT must be visible in all classes of the type.

Definition

Let $a \in A$ such that INIT is in A's visibility list.

$$a.\mathit{INIT} \Leftrightarrow [a.t_1/t_1, \ldots, a.t_n/t_n, a.x_1/x_1, \ldots, a.x_m/x_m] \ \textbf{subs init}(A)$$
$$\text{where } \textbf{types}(A) = \{t_1, \ldots, t_n\}$$
$$\textbf{vars}(\textbf{state}(A)) = \{x_1, \ldots, x_m\}$$

4.6 Expressions

Name

Class names

Description

A class name can be used as an expression representing the set of all identities of objects of the class. This set is either empty, when the class has no possible initial states, or countably infinite. The sets of object identities of distinct classes are disjoint. If the class has formal generic parameters then these must be instantiated by either a previously declared type or a formal generic parameter of the environment in which the expression appears. Some or all of the class's visible features may be renamed. Renaming has no affect on the object identities represented by the expression — it only affects the names used to access the features of identified objects.

Syntax

Expression ::= ClassName *[*ActualParameters*]* *[*RenameList*]*

Rules

The form of the actual parameters and rename list are as for an inherited class designator (page 82).

Definition

$$\textbf{init}(A) = \varnothing \Rightarrow A = \varnothing$$
$$\textbf{init}(A) \neq \varnothing \Rightarrow \exists\, s : \mathbb{N} \rightarrowtail\!\!\!\!\twoheadrightarrow A \bullet \text{true}$$
$$A \cap B = \varnothing \quad \text{where } A \text{ is distinct from } B$$
$$A[t_1, \ldots, t_n] \subseteq A[X_1, \ldots, X_n]$$
$$t_1 \neq t_{n+1} \vee \ldots \vee t_n \neq t_{2*n} \Rightarrow A[t_1, \ldots, t_n] \cap A[t_{n+1}, \ldots, t_{2*n}] = \varnothing$$
$$A[x_1 / y_1, \ldots, x_m / y_m, Op_{i+1} / Op_1, \ldots, Op_{i+j} / Op_j] = A$$
$$\textbf{visible}(A[t_1, \ldots, t_n][x_1 / y_1, \ldots, x_m / y_m, Op_{i+1} / Op_1, \ldots, Op_{i+j} / Op_j]) = \\ \quad [x_1 / y_1, \ldots, x_m / y_m, Op_{i+1} / Op_1, \ldots, Op_{i+j} / Op_j] \textbf{ subs} \\ \quad \textbf{visible}(A[X_1, \ldots, X_n])$$

All other meta-functions applied to a class name expression are as defined for an inherited class designator (page 82).

Note

For the purposes of the definitions in this chapter, we assume the existence of a base type of which all class types are subsets. This allows us to write expressions relating different classes or object identities of different classes.

Name

Polymorphism

Description

The polymorphism operator $\downarrow$ is used to define the set of object identities belonging to a given class or any one of its subclasses (defined either before or after the given class in the specification). It can only be applied to a class name expression where each subclass has the same formal generic parameters as the given class, and at least all of the visible features of the given class.

Syntax

Expression ::= $\downarrow$Expression

Rules

The expression must be a class name expression. All subclasses of the associated class must have the same formal generic parameters as it and include, for each of its visible features, an identically named visible feature. Furthermore, these common-named visible features must be type compatible and, in the case of operations, have identical auxiliary variables.

Definition

The definition assumes the existence of a base type of which all class types are subsets as discussed on page 109.

$$\downarrow A = A \cup A_1 \cup \ldots \cup A_n$$
$$\text{where } \mathbf{inherited}^{\sim}(\!|\ \{A\}\ |\!) = \{A_1, \ldots, A_n\}$$

Name

Class union

Description

The class union operator is used to define the set of object identities belonging to two or more classes.

Syntax

$$\mathsf{Expression} \ ::= \ \mathsf{Expression} \cup \mathsf{Expression}$$

Rules

The expressions must be class name expressions or class union expressions.

Definition

The definition assumes the existence of a base type of which all class types are subsets as discussed on page 109.

$$A_1 \bigcup \ldots \bigcup A_n = A_1 \cup \ldots \cup A_n$$

Name

Object containment

Description

The object containment notation enables the specification of a set of object identities identical to that of a given class name expression but such that identities declared from this set are distinct when they occur as attributes of distinct objects. In this way, the concept of an object being a component of another object — and only of that object — can be captured.

Syntax

Expression ::= Expression$_{©}$

Rules

The expression must be a class name expression.

Definition

An object cannot be directly contained within two distinct objects. An object cannot directly or indirectly contain itself.

$$A_{©} = A$$
$$a.x \in A_{©} \wedge b.x \in A_{©} \wedge a \neq b \Rightarrow a.x \neq b.x$$
$$a \in A \wedge s_n.a_n \in A_{©} \Rightarrow s_n.a_n \neq a$$
$$\text{where } s_1 = a$$
$$s_2 = s_1.a_1$$
$$\vdots$$
$$s_n = s_{n-1}.a_{n-1}$$

Name

Promoted attributes

Description

Attribute promotion is used to access the visible attributes of an identified object.

Syntax

Expression ::= Expression . Identifier

Rules

The expression must be an object identity and the identifier must be a visible attribute of the class of the identified object or the constant *self*. In the case where the type of the object identity is a polymorphic type or a class union and is not further qualified, the identifier must be a visible attribute which is common to all classes of the type or the constant *self*.

Definition

Promoted attributes are constrained by the property of the state of their class.

$$a \in A \Rightarrow [a.t_1/t_1, \ldots, a.t_n/t_n, a.x_1/x_1, \ldots, a.x_m/x_m] \ \textbf{subs state}(A)$$
$$\text{where } \textbf{types}(A) = \{t_1, \ldots, t_n\}$$
$$\textbf{vars}(\textbf{state}(A)) = \{x_1, \ldots, x_m\}$$

Name

Self

Description

The constant *self* enables the specification of objects which reference themselves.

Syntax

$$\mathsf{Expression} ::= \ self$$

Definition

$$a.self = a$$

5

Concurrent Systems

Concurrent systems are systems comprising a collection of independent components which may perform operations *concurrently* — that is, at the same instant of time. Examples include distributed systems and systems implemented in terms of parallel processes for reasons such as efficiency. Although concurrency is essentially an implementation issue, for many systems, even functionality at the highest level of abstraction is best specified in terms of concurrent components.

Traditionally, state-based specification languages such as Z have not been used for the specification of concurrent systems. This is partly because they lack a means of conveniently specifying systems in terms of components. The structuring of systems as collections of distinct, interacting objects inherent to object orientation, however, makes Object-Z well suited to modelling concurrent systems.

We have already seen an example of concurrent system specification in Object-Z — the multiplexer specification of Chapter 1. The three queues could, in an implementation of this specification, potentially operate in a concurrent fashion. For example, the queue $input_1$ could perform a $Join$ operation at the same instant as the queue $output$ performing a $Leave$ operation. This is evident from the fact that the state of the system after the two operations are performed is independent of the order in which they occurred. This fashion of modelling concurrency is referred to as *interleaving concurrency* — since the operations occurring concurrently are *interleaved* in an arbitrary order.

In order to specify that two operations, possibly from distinct objects, must synchronize, we make use of Object-Z's operation operators. In the multiplexer specification, the conjunction operator $\wedge$ is used to specify synchronization of the queue $source$ with the queues $input_1$ and $input_2$ in operations $Leave_1$ and $Leave_2$ respectively. Also, communication between objects and nondeterministic choice of operations can be specified using, respectively, the parallel composition operator $\|$ and the nondeterministic choice operator $[]$ as in the multiplexer operation $Transfer$.

In the multiplexer example, the number of concurrent components is known and fixed. In many cases, however, we wish to abstract away from the number of components in the specification and require that the number of components is variable rather than fixed. In this chapter, we present guidelines for specifying systems comprising such arbitrary and variable sized collections of objects. We refer to these collections as *aggregates*. The guidelines are illustrated at the end of the chapter by a small case study based on the card game Hearts.

5.1 Aggregation

Aggregates of objects occur in Object-Z specifications when we have a collection of similar components making up the system — for example, the exchanges of a telephone network or the processors of a multiprocessor system. Ideally, the number of components in such systems should be dealt with in the design and implementation of the system and left arbitrary in its specification. We may, in addition, also require that components be able to be added or removed from the system.

Such arbitrary and variable sized aggregates can be specified in Object-Z by sets of object references. The use of a reference semantics, as opposed to a value-based semantics, in Object-Z means that there is no possibility of distinct objects being identified in such a set — even when they have the same attribute values. Furthermore, when an operation is applied to an object in such a set, the set itself is unchanged and, hence, there is no need for framing schemas often used in Z to indicate that all elements but one in a set are unchanged.

To illustrate the use of aggregation in Object-Z, we specify a system of electronic diaries used by the members of a software engineering laboratory. Given basic types *Time* and *Event* representing the sets of all times and events respectively, we specify a diary as follows.

Diary

$$schedule, additions : Time \pfun Event$$

INIT

$$schedule = additions = \varnothing$$

AddEvent

$$\Delta(additions)$$
$$t? : Time$$
$$e? : Event$$

$$t? \notin \mathrm{dom}\, schedule \cup \mathrm{dom}\, additions$$
$$additions' = additions \cup \{(t?, e?)\}$$

Commit

$$\Delta(schedule, additions)$$

$$schedule' = schedule \cup additions$$
$$additions' = \varnothing$$

Abort

$$\Delta(additions)$$

$$additions' = \varnothing$$

The diary includes a schedule of events *schedule* and a set of additions to the schedule made by the user *additions*. Initially, both are empty and the user makes additions modelled by the operation *AddEvent*. Such additions must not clash with events already in the schedule or existing proposed additions. At any time, the user can decide to commit the current additions to the schedule or abort them modelled by the operations *Commit* and *Abort* respectively.

Each member of the software engineering laboratory has a dairy. In later sections, we will show how, through synchronization and communication, the dairies of individual members can be kept consistent. For now, we assume each laboratory member is solely responsible for his or her diary.

The laboratory is specified as follows. We specify the aggregate of diaries polymorphically in anticipation of the extensions to the example in the following sections.

Laboratory

$diaries : \mathbb{P} \downarrow Diary$

INIT

$diaries = \varnothing$

AddDiary

$\Delta(diaries)$
$d? : Diary$

$d? \notin diaries$
$d?.\mathrm{INIT}$
$diaries' = diaries \cup \{d?\}$

RemoveDiary

$\Delta(diaries)$
$d? : Diary$

$d? \in diaries$
$diaries' = diaries \setminus \{d?\}$

$AddEvent \mathrel{\widehat=} [d : diaries] \bullet d.AddEvent$
$Commit \mathrel{\widehat=} [d : diaries] \bullet d.Commit$
$Abort \mathrel{\widehat=} [d : diaries] \bullet d.Abort$

Initially, the aggregate *diaries* is empty. The operations *AddDiary* and *RemoveDiary* allow diaries to be added and removed, respectively, as members join and leave the laboratory. Each user can add an event to his or her diary modelled by the operation *AddEvent*, and commit and abort additions modelled by the operations *Commit* and *Abort* respectively.

The latter three operations illustrate the use of the scope operator • for specifying operations on individual objects in aggregates. In general, one or more object references can be declared in the operation on the left-hand side of the scope operator and used in an operation expression on its right-hand side. Note that these operations have an empty Δ-list and do not change the attribute *diaries*.

5.2 Synchronization

When systems are designed and implemented in terms of concurrently operating components, the usual intention is that the components will in some way interact. Such interaction occurs when distinct components undergo operations simultaneously. This is referred to as *synchronization*.

In Object-Z synchronization can be expressed using the conjunction operator $\wedge$. That is, given object identities a and b, to specify that the object identified by a undergoes an operation OpA in synchronization with the object identified by b undergoing an operation OpB we write $a.OpA \wedge b.OpB$.

When dealing with aggregates of objects, the distributed conjunction operator is often useful since we may want to specify that all objects in the aggregate, or some subset of it, undergo a particular operation. This is illustrated by the following extensions to the diaries example.

$$\textit{Diary}1$$
$$\textit{Diary}$$
$$request : Time \pfun Event$$
$$\textsc{Init}$$
$$request = \varnothing$$
$$ReceiveRequest$$
$$\Delta(request)$$
$$r? : Time \pfun Event$$
$$request = \varnothing$$
$$request' = r?$$
$$CommitRequest$$
$$\Delta(schedule, request)$$
$$(\operatorname{dom} schedule \cup \operatorname{dom} additions) \cap \operatorname{dom} request = \varnothing$$
$$schedule' = schedule \cup request$$
$$request' = \varnothing$$
$$AbortRequest$$
$$\Delta(request)$$
$$request' = \varnothing$$

As well as additions made by the user of the diary, the diary may receive external requests for events to be added to the schedule. These requests may, for example, be from the laboratory's coordinator in order to schedule meetings. As with additions made by the user, the user may decide to commit or abort such requests. He or she can only commit a request when it does not lead to a clash with either the schedule or existing proposed additions.

We assume that such requests are broadcast to all members of the laboratory. Furthermore, so that individual diaries are kept consistent, a user can only commit, or abort, a request when all other users do the same. This situation is specified by the class *Laboratory*1.

$$
\begin{array}{l}
\underline{\mathit{Laboratory}1} \\
\mathit{Laboratory} \\
\hline
\mathit{diaries} : \mathbb{P}\, \mathit{Diary}1 \\
\hline
\mathit{Request} \mathrel{\widehat{=}} \bigwedge d : \mathit{diaries} \bullet d.\mathit{ReceiveRequest} \\
\mathit{CommitRequest} \mathrel{\widehat{=}} \bigwedge d : \mathit{diaries} \bullet d.\mathit{CommitRequest} \\
\mathit{AbortRequest} \mathrel{\widehat{=}} \bigwedge d : \mathit{diaries} \bullet d.\mathit{AbortRequest}
\end{array}
$$

The operation *Request* specifies a request being broadcast to all members of the laboratory. The operations *CommitRequest* and *AbortRequest* specify all members of the laboratory committing or aborting a request respectively. The actual mechanism by which such synchronization is achieved is not presented at this level of abstraction. For example, it may involve all members of the laboratory acknowledging the request by a vote and then, if one or more votes is negative, the broadcast of an abort order or, otherwise, a commit order.

5.3 Communication

One of the main uses of synchronization is to allow concurrent components to communicate information. In Object-Z communication is modelled using the parallel composition operator $\|$. To illustrate this, we extend the diary example again.

$$
\begin{array}{l}
\underline{\mathit{Diary}2} \\
\mathit{Diary}1 \\
\quad \underline{\mathit{SendRequest}} \\
\quad \Delta(\mathit{additions}, \mathit{request}) \\
\quad r! : \mathit{Time} \mathrel{+\!\!\!\!\twoheadrightarrow} \mathit{Event} \\
\quad \hline
\quad \mathit{request} = \varnothing \\
\quad r! = \mathit{additions} \\
\quad \mathit{additions}' = \varnothing \\
\quad \mathit{request}' = \mathit{additions}
\end{array}
$$

The operation *SendRequest* outputs the additions made by the user of a diary and moves the additions to the diary's *request* variable. This places the diary in the same state as if it had received a request. It can therefore participate in the decision to commit or abort the request along with the other laboratory members. This behaviour is captured by the class *Laboratory2*.

$$
\begin{array}{|l}
\textit{Laboratory2} \\
\hline
\textit{Laboratory} \\
\quad \boxed{\textit{diaries} : \mathbb{P}\,\textit{Diary2}} \\
\textit{Request} \mathrel{\widehat{=}} [\, c : \textit{diaries} \,] \bullet \\
\qquad (c.\textit{SendRequest} \parallel (\bigwedge d : \textit{diaries} \setminus \{c\} \bullet d.\textit{ReceiveRequest})) \\
\textit{CommitRequest} \mathrel{\widehat{=}} \bigwedge d : \textit{diaries} \bullet d.\textit{CommitRequest} \\
\textit{AbortRequest} \mathrel{\widehat{=}} \bigwedge d : \textit{diaries} \bullet d.\textit{AbortRequest} \\
\hline
\end{array}
$$

The operation *Request* models a single diary c, belonging to the coordinator of the request, sending a request in parallel with all other members of the laboratory receiving the request. The operations for committing or aborting the request are as in *Laboratory1*.

As well as $\parallel$, the associative version of the parallel composition operator $\parallel_!$ and the sequential composition operator $⨾$, in both its binary and distributed forms, may be useful for modelling communication. Since $\parallel_!$ does not hide the communicated values, it may be necessary to use it in conjunction with the hiding operator. Its advantage over the other operators is that it enables three, or more, operations to be composed such that each can receive all communications from the others.

Since communication is only effected by any of these operators when there are inputs and outputs with matching basenames, it is often useful to use them in combination with renaming. For example, given that Op_1 has an output $x!$ which we wish to communicate with an input $y?$ of operation Op_2 we write $Op_1 \parallel Op_2[x?/y?]$.

5.4 Nondeterminism

Synchronization and communication allow the components of a concurrent system to influence the behaviour of other components. However, components are also capable of choosing between the possible behaviours they can undergo independently of their environment. For example, a telephone exchange may divert certain calls to different exchanges depending on the time of day. The other exchanges have no way of influencing this behaviour nor of even observing the decisions being made as to which exchange the calls should be diverted to. Such nondeterminism is referred to as *internal* nondeterminism.

In Object-Z, internal nondeterminism can be modelled using the nondeterministic choice operator $[]$. To illustrate this, we again extend the diaries example. Since not all members of the diary need attend every meeting, we allow a user to ignore a request.

This is different from the user committing — so as not to cause a meeting he or she is not interested in to be aborted — as it allows his or her diary to have events which clash with the request.

$$
\begin{array}{|l}
\hline
\textit{Diary3} \\
\hline
\textit{Diary2} \\
\quad \begin{array}{|l}
\hline
\textit{Ignore} \\
\hline
\Delta(\textit{request}) \\
\hline
\textit{request}' = \varnothing \\
\hline
\end{array} \\
\hline
\end{array}
$$

The laboratory is respecified as follows.

$$
\begin{array}{|l}
\hline
\textit{Laboratory3} \\
\hline
\textit{Laboratory} \\
\begin{array}{|l}
\hline
\textit{diaries} : \mathbb{P}\,\textit{Diary3} \\
\hline
\end{array} \\
\textit{Request} \mathrel{\widehat=} [\, c : \textit{diaries} \,] \bullet \\
\qquad (c.\textit{SendRequest} \parallel (\bigwedge d : \textit{diaries} \setminus \{c\} \bullet d.\textit{ReceiveRequest})) \\
\textit{CommitRequest} \mathrel{\widehat=} \bigwedge d : \textit{diaries} \bullet (d.\textit{CommitRequest} \sqcap d.\textit{Ignore}) \\
\textit{AbortRequest} \mathrel{\widehat=} \bigwedge d : \textit{diaries} \bullet (d.\textit{AbortRequest} \sqcap d.\textit{Ignore}) \\
\hline
\end{array}
$$

The operation *Request* is as in *Laboratory2*. The operations *CommitRequest* and *AbortRequest* now allow each member of the laboratory to ignore any request. The choice to participate in the acceptance of the request or to simply ignore it is made internally and is not influenced by the choices of other members. This abstract representation of the choice at the system level would, in practice, be refined to a single operation of the class *Diary3*.

The distributed version of the nondeterministic choice operator is also useful for specifying a choice between components which cannot be influenced by the environment of a concurrent system. For example, the *RemoveDiary* operation of the laboratory could be redefined as follows.

$$\textit{RemoveDiary} \mathrel{\widehat=} \bigsqcap d : \textit{diaries} \bullet [\Delta(\textit{diaries}) \mid \textit{diaries}' = \textit{diaries} \setminus \{d\}]$$

The diary to be removed is now not input from the environment but chosen internally. Note that there is a subtle difference between this definition and the following.

$$\textit{RemoveDiary} \mathrel{\widehat=} [\, d : \textit{diaries} \,] \bullet [\Delta(\textit{diaries}) \mid \textit{diaries}' = \textit{diaries} \setminus \{d\}]$$

This second definition represents a choice which can be influenced externally since, given $\textit{lab} : \textit{Laboratory}$, d may be further constrained by operations conjoined with $\textit{lab}.\textit{RemoveDiary}$. Unlike internal nondeterminism, the nondeterminism in such operations cannot be reduced during refinement.

5.5 Case Study: Hearts

To illustrate the specification of concurrent systems involving aggregates of objects, we present, in this section, a small case study based on the card game Hearts. The system we specify comprises a number of computer terminals via which players can participate in the game.

Hearts is a trick taking game played by three of more players. A trick is a set of cards of which one card is contributed by each player. One of the players leads — that is, plays the first card of the trick — by placing a card from his or her hand face up on the table. The other players, in turn, add a card from their hands to the trick following the suit of the first card when this is possible — that is, if the first card was of the suit Clubs, each player must play a Club if he or she holds a Club, otherwise the player can play any card. When all players have played, the player who played the highest card of the same suit as the first card wins the trick.

Normally, the objective of Hearts is not to win tricks which contain any Hearts or the Queen of Spades. For each Heart won the player receives one point. For the Queen of Spades the player receives 13 points. Each time the players run out of cards, the points in the tricks they have won are added to their scores and the cards are redealt. This continues until at least one player's score is greater than 100 at which time the player with the lowest score is declared the winner.

An alternative strategy to not winning tricks containing Hearts or the Queen of Spades is to win all such tricks — this is referred to as "shooting the moon". Then, when the players run out of cards, the player with all the points may choose either to reduce his or her score by 26 points, or to have all other players' scores increased by 26.

Each player in our specification sits in front of a screen which displays his or her hand of cards, the cards in the current trick being played and the scores of each player. A typical snapshot is shown below.

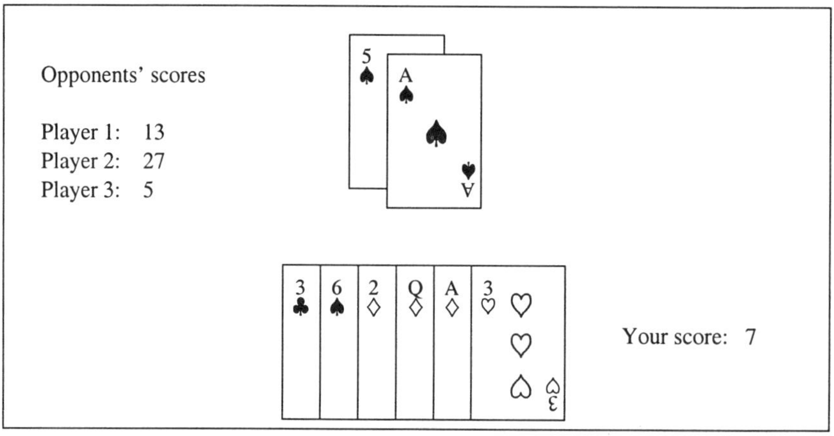

Figure 5.1: Hearts screen

We begin the specification by specifying the types *Suit* and *Value* representing the possible suits and values of cards respectively.

$$\begin{aligned} Suit &::= Clubs \mid Spades \mid Diamonds \mid Hearts \\ Value &::= number\langle\langle 2\,..\,10 \rangle\rangle \mid Jack \mid Queen \mid King \mid Ace \end{aligned}$$

The type *Card* denoting the set of all cards is defined as follows.

$$Card == Suit \times Value$$

For convenience, we also define the following functions which return the suit and value of a card.

$$\begin{array}{|l} suit\_of : Card \rightarrow Suit \\ value\_of : Card \rightarrow Value \\ \hline \forall s : Suit;\ v : Value \bullet \\ \quad suit\_of(s, v) = s \land \\ \quad value\_of(s, v) = v \end{array}$$

We make use of inheritance to specify the game of Hearts incrementally. We begin by specifying an abstract class *CardPlayer* which can be used in the specification of other card games as well as Hearts. Its state comprises a set of opponents — other card players — and a set of cards denoting the player's hand.

CardPlayer

$$\begin{array}{|l} opponents : \mathbb{P} \downarrow CardPlayer \\ hand : \mathbb{P}\ Card \\ \hline self \notin opponents \end{array}$$

INIT

$$\begin{array}{|l} hand = \varnothing \end{array}$$

OpponentJoins

$$\begin{array}{|l} \Delta(opponents) \\ p? : (\downarrow CardPlayer) \setminus opponents \\ \hline opponents' = opponents \cup \{p?\} \end{array}$$

ReceiveDeal

$$\begin{array}{|l} \Delta(hand) \\ cards? : \mathbb{P}\ Card \\ \hline hand = \varnothing \\ hand' = cards? \end{array}$$

The set of opponents is specified polymorphically in anticipation of the use of subclasses of *CardPlayer* in the specification of specific card games such as Hearts. Undesirable aliasing caused by *CardPlayer*'s recursive structure is avoided by ensuring a player's identity is not included in the set of opponents.

Initially, the player's hand is empty. An initial value is not specified for the set of opponents as other players may have previously joined the game. The operation *OpponentJoins* corresponds to an opponent joining the game and *ReceiveDeal* to a hand being dealt to the player.

A card game is specified as an aggregate of players. Players may continue to join the game until it is started when the cards are dealt.

CardGame

$$\upharpoonright(players, cards, \mathit{INIT}, Join, ReceiveDeal, Redeal)$$

$$players : \mathbb{P} \downarrow CardPlayer$$
$$cards : \mathbb{P}\, Card$$

INIT

$$players = \varnothing$$
$$cards = Card$$

NewPlayer

$$\Delta(players)$$
$$p? : \downarrow CardPlayer$$

$$cards = Card$$
$$p?.\mathit{INIT}$$
$$p?.opponents = players$$
$$players' = players \cup \{p?\}$$

AllocateCards

$$\Delta(cards)$$
$$cards! : \mathbb{P}\, cards$$

$$\#cards! = \#Card \operatorname{div} \#players$$
$$cards' = cards \setminus cards!$$

$$Join \mathrel{\widehat=} NewPlayer \wedge (\textstyle\bigwedge p : players \bullet p.OpponentJoins)$$
$$Deal \mathrel{\widehat=} \mathbin{⨟} p : players \bullet AllocateCards \parallel p.ReceiveDeal$$
$$Redeal \mathrel{\widehat=} [\Delta(cards) \mid cards \neq Card \wedge cards' = Card] \mathbin{⨟} Deal$$

The set of players of a card game is denoted by the variable *players* and the set of cards not currently dealt to any player by the variable *cards*. The latter variable is not associated with any of the concurrent components. Such variables are often useful for specifying concurrent systems at a high level of abstraction as they allow constraints about the whole system to be captured. This can be used to reduce the number of concurrent components in the high-level specification, or to simplify the state and behaviour of specified components. For example, an implementation of

CardGame would require the information modelled by *cards* to be incorporated in either an additional coordinating component, or in each of the player components. In the latter case, the *cards* variable would be replicated in each of the players and consistency of its value maintained through synchronization.

Initially, the set of players is empty and no cards have been dealt — that is, $cards = Card$. The visibility list of *CardGame* indicates that the operations *NewPlayer* and *AllocateCards* are not in the class's interface. These operations cannot, therefore, occur in isolation. They can occur, however, in synchronization with operations of the players.

The operation *NewPlayer* enables a new player to be added to the set *players* provided the game has not started — indicated by the fact that no cards have been dealt. The new player must be in an initial state and its set of opponents must be the current set of players of the game. To ensure all players recognize the new player, this operation can only occur in synchronization with all players performing an *OpponentJoins* operation as specified by the visible operation *Join*.

The operation *AllocateCards* models a set of cards being allocated to a player and removed from *cards*. The predicate ensures that each player gets the same number of cards equal to the the total number of cards divided by the number of players (the cards constituting any remainder are not dealt). This operation is used in the visible operations *Deal* and *Redeal*.

The operation *Deal* models each player in *players* receiving a distinct set of cards. This is specified by each player performing the *ReceiveDeal* operation of *CardPlayer* in synchronization with *AllocateCards*. Communication is effected by the use of the parallel composition operator. Since *AllocateCards* changes the variable *cards* from which the allocated cards are drawn, the operation is specified using the distributed sequential composition operator.

The operation *Redeal* models the cards being redealt after the game has already started — indicated by the fact that some cards have been dealt. It is specified as the sequential composition of an operation which returns the dealt cards to the set *cards*, and the operation *Deal*.

We continue our specification by specializing the classes *CardPlayer* and *CardGame* for trick taking games. As a preliminary, we define the relation *higher_than* which relates each card value to those values higher than it.

$$higher\_than : Value \leftrightarrow Value$$

$$\begin{array}{l}
\forall n_1, n_2 : 2 \,..\, 10 \bullet number(n_1) \ \underline{higher_than} \ number(n_2) \Leftrightarrow n_1 > n_2 \\
\forall v_1 : Value;\ v_2 : Value \setminus \operatorname{ran} number \bullet \\
\quad v_2 \ \underline{higher_than} \ v_1 \Leftrightarrow \\
\qquad (v_1 \in \operatorname{ran} number \\
\qquad \lor v_1 = Jack \land v_2 \in \{Queen, King, Ace\} \\
\qquad \lor v_1 = Queen \land v_2 \in \{King, Ace\} \\
\qquad \lor v_1 = King \land v_2 = Ace)
\end{array}$$

Let $Trick == \operatorname{seq} Card$ denote the set of all tricks. The player of a tricks taking game is specified by the class *TricksPlayer*.

TricksPlayer

CardPlayer

$$opponents : \mathbb{P} \downarrow TricksPlayer$$
$$tricks : \mathbb{P}\, Trick$$
$$trick : Trick$$
$$played : \mathbb{P}\, Card$$

$$\#played \leqslant 1$$

INIT

$$tricks = \varnothing$$
$$trick = \langle\rangle$$
$$played = \varnothing$$

Play

$$\Delta(hand, trick, played)$$
$$card! : hand$$

$$played = \varnothing$$
$$trick \neq \langle\rangle \wedge suit\_of(trick(1)) \in suit\_of(\!|\, hand \,|\!) \Rightarrow$$
$$\quad suit\_of(card!) = suit\_of(trick(1))$$
$$hand' = hand \setminus \{card!\}$$
$$trick' = trick \frown \langle card! \rangle$$
$$played' = \{card!\}$$

OpponentPlays

$$\Delta(trick)$$
$$card? : Card$$

$$trick' = trick \frown \langle card? \rangle$$

TakeTrick

$$\Delta(trick, played, tricks)$$

$$\exists\, c_1 : played \mid suit\_of(c_1) = suit\_of(trick(1)) \bullet$$
$$\quad \forall\, c_2 : \{suit\_of(trick(1))\} \lhd (\operatorname{ran} trick \setminus \{c_1\}) \bullet$$
$$\qquad value\_of(c_1)\ \underline{higher\_than}\ value\_of(c_2)$$
$$tricks' = tricks \cup \{trick\}$$
$$trick' = \langle\rangle$$
$$played' = \varnothing$$

OpponentTakesTrick

$$\Delta(trick, played)$$

$$played \neq \varnothing$$
$$trick' = \langle\rangle$$
$$played' = \varnothing$$

The class *TricksPlayer* is a subclass of *CardPlayer*. The state variable *tricks* denotes the set of tricks won by the player and the state variable *trick* denotes the current trick being played. Initially, both are empty.

The state variable *played* denotes the card played by the player in the current trick. It is represented by a set of cards which is either empty or has one element. Initially, it is empty. The variable is used for two purposes: to indicate whether a player can play a card — this can only be done when *played* is empty — and to indicate whether a player can take a trick — this can only be done when *played* is the highest card of the suit of the leading card of the trick.

The playing of a card is modelled by the operation *Play*. The predicate ensures that the card played is of the suit of the leading card of the current trick when this is possible. The played card is removed from the player's hand and added to the trick and to the set *played*. Cards may also be played by other players as modelled by the operation *OpponentPlays*.

The taking of a trick is modelled by the operation *TakeTrick*. The predicate ensures that a player only takes a trick when he or she has played a card of the same suit as the leading card and, furthermore, that his or her card is the highest of that suit in the trick. The trick is added to the player's set of won tricks and *trick* and *played* are made empty in order that another trick may be played. Another player may also take a trick as modelled by the operation *OpponentTakesTrick*. Note that this operation can only occur when the player has played a card.

Whenever one player plays a card — operation *Play* — all other players need to add this card to their copy of the current trick — operation *OpponentPlays*. Similarly, whenever a player takes a trick — operation *TakeTrick* — all other players need to set their their copy of the trick and their *played* variable to empty in order to play the next trick — operation *OpponentTakesTrick*. This behaviour is specified by the following class *TricksGame*.

TricksGame

$\upharpoonright(players, cards, \mathrm{INIT}, Join, Deal, Redeal, Play, TakeTrick)$

$CardGame$

$players : \mathbb{P}{\downarrow}TricksPlayer$

$$Play \mathrel{\widehat{=}} [p : players] \bullet p.Play \parallel (\bigwedge q : players \setminus \{p\} \bullet q.OpponentPlays)$$

$$TakeTrick \mathrel{\widehat{=}} [p : players] \bullet p.TakeTrick \wedge (\bigwedge q : players \setminus \{p\} \bullet q.OpponentTakesTrick)$$

The class *TricksGame* is a subclass of *CardGame* with two additional visible operations — *Play* and *TakeTrick* — modelling the playing of a card and taking of a trick respectively.

To complete the specification of the game of Hearts we need to add to *TricksGame* the details of scoring. The order in which players play a card has also not been specified but will be ignored for the purposes of this case study — the specification can be thought of as an abstract representation of the game into which these details could be later added.

To add the details of scoring, we extend the player and game classes again using inheritance. As a preliminary, we introduce a function *points* which returns the number of points in a set of tricks.

$$points : \mathbb{P}\, Trick \rightarrow \mathbb{N}$$

$$\begin{array}{l} \forall\, tricks : \mathbb{P}\, Trick;\ cards : \mathbb{P}\, Card;\ hearts : \mathbb{N} \bullet \\ \quad (cards = \operatorname{ran} {}^\frown/\, tricks \land \\ \quad hearts = \#(\{Hearts\} \lhd cards)) \Rightarrow \\ \qquad (Spades, Queen) \notin cards \Rightarrow points(tricks) = hearts \land \\ \qquad (Spades, Queen) \in cards \Rightarrow points(tricks) = hearts + 13 \end{array}$$

In the above definition, *cards* represents the set of cards and *hearts* the number of cards of suit Hearts in a set of tricks denoted by *tricks*. If the Queen of Spades is not included in *cards* then the points of *tricks* is equal to *hearts*. If the Queen of Spades is included in *cards* then an additional 13 points is included in *tricks*.

To consistently update the scores at each player's terminal in our system requires communication of the points won by each player to each other player. This could be specified as a number of broadcast operations — one for each player. Alternatively, it can be specified at a higher level of abstraction by a single operation in which all players synchronize and produce a common output detailing the new scores of all players. Each player partially restricts this output depending on the points in the tricks that he or she has won.

To facilitate specifying the class of such a player, we define a schema *UpdateScores* as an abbreviation of a set of declarations and predicates common to all operations for updating the players' scores.

UpdateScores

$$\begin{array}{l} hand : \mathbb{P}\, Card \\ trick : Trick \\ tricks' : \mathbb{P}\, Trick \\ score' : HeartsPlayer \rightarrow\!\!\!\!\!\!+ \mathbb{N} \\ new\_score! : HeartsPlayer \rightarrow\!\!\!\!\!\!+ \mathbb{N} \end{array}$$

$$\begin{array}{l} hand = \varnothing \\ trick = \langle\rangle \\ tricks' = \varnothing \\ score' = new\_score! \end{array}$$

The schema includes a precondition that the player's hand and the current trick are empty — that is, all cards have been played and the final trick has been taken — and a postcondition that the set of tricks the player has won becomes empty, and the scores of all players is updated according to the output variable $new\_scores!$.

A player of the game of Hearts is specified by the class $HeartsPlayer$.

HeartsPlayer

$TricksPlayer$

$$opponents : \mathbb{P}\, HeartsPlayer$$
$$score : HeartsPlayer \rightarrow\!\!\!\!\!\!+\ \mathbb{N}$$

$$\mathrm{dom}\, score = opponents \cup \{self\}$$

INIT

$$\forall p : \mathrm{dom}\, score \bullet score(p) = 0$$

OpponentJoins

$$\Delta(score)$$

$$score' = score \cup \{p? \mapsto 0\}$$

Score

$$\Delta(score)$$
$$UpdateScores$$

$$points(tricks) \neq 26$$
$$(new\_score!(self) = score(self) + points(tricks)$$
$$\vee$$
$$points(tricks) = 0 \wedge$$
$$(\exists p : opponents \bullet$$
$$\quad new\_score!(p) = score(p) \wedge$$
$$\quad (\forall q : \mathrm{dom}\, score \setminus \{p\} \bullet$$
$$\qquad new\_score!(q) = score(q) + 26)))$$

ReduceScore

$$\Delta(score)$$
$$UpdateScores$$

$$points(tricks) = 26$$
$$new\_score!(self) = score(self) - 26$$

IncreaseOpponentsScores

$$\Delta(score)$$
$$UpdateScores$$

$$points(tricks) = 26$$
$$new\_score!(self) = score(self)$$
$$\forall p : opponents \bullet new\_score!(p) = score(p) + 26$$

The class *HeartsPlayer* is a subclass of *TricksPlayer* with an additional state variable *score* denoting the scores of the player and his or her opponents. Initially, all scores are zero and if a new opponent joins the game he or she is given a score of zero.

The scores can be updated in three ways.

1. If the player has not won all the Hearts and the Queen of Spades and, therefore, has less than 26 points, his or her score is either increased by his or her points, or by 26. In the former case, the scores of all other players are left undetermined. In the latter — corresponding to an opponent "shooting the moon" — a single opponent's score is unchanged and all others are increased by 26. This is modelled by the operation *Score*.
2. If the player has won all the Hearts and the Queen of Spades and, therefore, has 26 points, he or she may decide to decrease his or her score by 26. This is modelled by the operation *ReduceScore*.
3. Alternatively, if the player has won all the Hearts and the Queen of Spades, he or she may decide to increase all other players' scores by 26. This is modelled by the operation *IncreaseOpponentsScores*.

The game of Hearts is specified as a subclass of *TricksGame* in which the players are of class *HeartsPlayer* and their scores can be updated either by each player concurrently performing the operation *Score* or one player "shooting the moon" — performing either the operation *ReduceScore* or *IncreaseOpponentsScores* — in synchronization with all other players performing *Score*.

HeartsGame

$\upharpoonright(players, cards, \mathrm{INIT}, Join, Deal, Redeal, Play, TakeTrick,$
$\quad Score, ShootTheMoon)$

TricksGame

$players : \mathbb{P}\, HeartsPlayer$

$Score \mathrel{\widehat=} \bigwedge p : players \bullet p.Score$

$$ShootTheMoon \mathrel{\widehat=} [p : players] \bullet (p.ReduceScore \;[]\; p.IncreaseOpponentsScores) \wedge (\bigwedge q : players \setminus \{p\} \bullet q.Score)$$

The operation *Score* models the case where all the Hearts and the Queen of Spades are not won by a single player. The common output $new\_scores!$ is restricted by the distributed conjunction so that the score of each player is increased by his or her points.

The operation *ShootTheMoon* models the case where all the Hearts and the Queen of Spades are won by a single player p. This player can decide to either reduce his or her score or to increase those of all other players. This decision is specified in terms of the nondeterministic choice operator to model the fact that it is internal and is not affected by the player's opponents.

6

Concrete Syntax

The concrete syntax of Object-Z extends that of Z with productions for class paragraphs and their associated definitions — visibility lists, inherited class designators, state schemas, initial state schemas and operations. In addition, the productions for predicates are extended to include initial state predicate promotions and (Boolean-valued) expressions, and the productions for expressions are extended to include class names, expressions involving polymorphism, class union and object containment, attribute promotion and the constant *self*.

This chapter presents the full concrete syntax of Object-Z in a top-down fashion. The syntax is described using an extended BNF based on that used for the syntax of Z in J.M. Spivey's *The Z Notation* (Prentice Hall, 1989 & 1992). Lists of one of more instances of a particular construct are denoted using ellipses. For example, a vertical list of one or more paragraphs is denoted

Paragraph
⋮
Paragraph

and a horizontal list of identifiers as

Identifier, . . . , Identifier

In the latter case, the identifiers are separated by commas. Optional constructs are enclosed by slanted square brackets *[ ]*.

The precedence of operation operators, schema operators and logical operators is indicated by the order in which they appear. Each operator binds tighter than those it precedes. The association of these operators is indicated by an upper-case letter at the right margin — 'L' indicates that the operator is left-associative, 'R' indicates that the operator is right associative and 'U' indicates that it is a unary operator.

The same upper-case letters are also used to indicate the associativity of infix generic names — that is, names of generic infix symbols such as $\leftrightarrow$ and $\nrightarrow$ — and infix function names — that is, names of infix function symbols such as $+$ and $\cup$. Infix generic symbols all have equal binding power. The precedence of infix function symbols is indicated by a number from one to six at the right margin with higher numbers representing tighter binding.

6.1 Specifications

```
Specification          ::= Paragraph
                            ⋮
                           Paragraph
```

6.2 Global Paragraphs

```
Paragraph              ::= BasicTypeDefinition
                         | AxiomaticDefinition
                         | GenericDefinition
                         | AbbreviationDefinition
                         | FreeTypeDefinition
                         | Schema
                         | Class
                         | Predicate

BasicTypeDefinition    ::= [Identifier, ..., Identifier]

AxiomaticDefinition    ::=    | Declaration
                           [  |------------
                              | PredicateList]

GenericDefinition      ::=    ╒═ [FormalParameters] ═══════════════
                              | Declaration
                           [  |------------
                              | PredicateList]
                              └─────────────────────────────────────

AbbreviationDefinition ::= Abbreviation == Expression

Abbreviation           ::= VariableName [FormalParameters]
                         | PrefixGenericName Identifier
                         | Identifier InfixGenericName Identifier

FreeTypeDefinition     ::= Identifier ::= Branch | ... | Branch

Branch                 ::= Identifier
                         | VariableName⟨⟨Expression⟩⟩

Schema                 ::=    ┌─SchemaHeader──────────────────────
                              | Declaration
                           [  |------------
                              | PredicateList]
                              └─────────────────────────────────────

                         | SchemaHeader ≙ SchemaExpression
```

```
SchemaHeader        ::=  SchemaName [FormalParameters]

Class               ::=  ┌─ClassName [FormalParameters] ─────────
                         │ [VisibilityList]
                         │ [InheritedClass
                         │   ⋮
                         │  InheritedClass]
                         │ [LocalDefinition
                         │   ⋮
                         │  LocalDefinition]
                         │ [State]
                         │ [InitialState]
                         │ [Operation
                         │   ⋮
                         │  Operation]
                         └──────────────────────────────────────

SchemaName          ::=  Word

ClassName           ::=  Word

FormalParameters    ::=  [Identifier, ..., Identifier]
```

6.3 Class Paragraphs

```
VisibilityList      ::=  ↾(DeclarationNameList)

InheritedClass      ::=  ClassName [ActualParameters] [RenameList]

LocalDefinition     ::=  BasicTypeDefinition
                      |  AxiomaticDefinition
                      |  AbbreviationDefinition
                      |  FreeTypeDefinition

State               ::=     ┌──────────────────────────────────
                            │ Declaration
                            │ [Δ
                            │  Declaration]
                          [ ├──────────
                            │ PredicateList]
                            └──────────────────────────────────
```

```
            |      ┌─────────────────────────────
                   │ Δ
                   │ Declaration
                 [ ├──────────
                   │ PredicateList]
                   └─────────────────────────────

            |      ┌─────────────────────────────
                   │ PredicateList
                   └─────────────────────────────

            |  [Declaration [Δ Declaration] [ | Predicate] ]

            |  [Δ Declaration [ | Predicate] ]

            |  [Predicate]

                   ┌─INIT────────────────────────
InitialState  ::=  │ PredicateList
                   └─────────────────────────────

            |  INIT ≙ [Predicate]

                   ┌─OperationName───────────────
Operation     ::=  │ DeltaList
                   │ [Declaration]
                 [ ├──────────
                   │ PredicateList]
                   └─────────────────────────────
                   ┌─OperationName───────────────
            |      │ Declaration
                 [ ├──────────
                   │ PredicateList]
                   └─────────────────────────────
                   ┌─OperationName───────────────
            |      │ [PredicateList]
                   └─────────────────────────────

            |  OperationName ≙ OperationExpression
```

OperationName ::= Identifier

DeltaList ::= Δ(DeclarationNameList)

6.4 Operation Expressions

```
OperationExpression ::= ⋀ Declaration [ | Predicate] • OperationExpression
                      | [] Declaration [ | Predicate] • OperationExpression
                      | ⨟ Declaration [ | Predicate] • OperationExpression
                      | OperationExpression1
```

OperationExpression1	::=	[DeltaList [Declaration] [$\mid$ Predicate]]	
	$\mid$	[Declaration [$\mid$ Predicate]]	
	$\mid$	[[Predicate]]	
	$\mid$	Expression . Identifier [RenameList]	
	$\mid$	Identifier [RenameList]	
	$\mid$	OperationExpression1 $\setminus$ (DeclarationNameList)	L
	$\mid$	OperationExpression1 $\wedge$ OperationExpression1	L
	$\mid$	OperationExpression1 $\parallel$ OperationExpression1	L
	$\mid$	OperationExpression1 $\parallel_!$ OperationExpression1	L
	$\mid$	OperationExpression1 $[]$ OperationExpression1	L
	$\mid$	OperationExpression1 $\fatsemi$ OperationExpression1	L
	$\mid$	OperationExpression1 $\bullet$ OperationExpression1	L
	$\mid$	(OperationExpression)	

6.5 Schema Expressions

SchemaExpression	::=	$\forall$ SchemaText $\bullet$ SchemaExpression	
	$\mid$	$\exists$ SchemaText $\bullet$ SchemaExpression	
	$\mid$	$\exists_1$ SchemaText $\bullet$ SchemaExpression	
	$\mid$	SchemaExpression1	
SchemaExpression1	::=	[SchemaText]	
	$\mid$	SchemaReference	
	$\mid$	$\neg$ SchemaExpression1	U
	$\mid$	pre SchemaExpression1	U
	$\mid$	SchemaExpression1 $\wedge$ SchemaExpression1	L
	$\mid$	SchemaExpression1 $\vee$ SchemaExpression1	L
	$\mid$	SchemaExpression1 $\Rightarrow$ SchemaExpression1	R
	$\mid$	SchemaExpression1 $\Leftrightarrow$ SchemaExpression1	L
	$\mid$	SchemaExpression1 $\upharpoonright$ SchemaExpression1	L
	$\mid$	SchemaExpression1 $\setminus$ (DeclarationNameList)	L
	$\mid$	SchemaExpression1 $\fatsemi$ SchemaExpression1	L
	$\mid$	SchemaExpression1 $>>$ SchemaExpression1	L
	$\mid$	(SchemaExpression)	
SchemaText	::=	Declaration [$\mid$ Predicate]	
SchemaReference	::=	SchemaReference1 [RenameList]	
SchemaReference1	::=	SchemaName Decoration [ActualParameters]	
RenameList	::=	[RenameItem , ... , RenameItem]	
RenameItem	::=	DeclarationName/DeclarationName	
ActualParameters	::=	[Expression , ... , Expression]	

6.6 Declarations

Declaration	::=	BasicDeclaration ; . . . ; BasicDeclaration
	|	Declaration ⋮ Declaration
BasicDeclaration	::=	DeclarationNameList : Expression
	|	SchemaReference
DeclarationNameList	::=	DeclarationName , . . . , DeclarationName
DeclarationName	::=	Identifier
	|	OperatorName

6.7 Predicates

PredicateList	::=	Predicate;. . . ;Predicate	
	|	PredicateList ⋮ PredicateList	
Predicate	::=	∀ SchemaText • Predicate	
	|	∃ SchemaText • Predicate	
	|	$\exists_1$ SchemaText • Predicate	
	|	**let** LetDefinition ; . . . ; LetDefinition • Predicate	
	|	Predicate1	
Predicate1	::=	Expression Relation . . . Relation Expression	
	|	PrefixRelationName Expression	
	|	SchemaReference	
	|	pre SchemaReference	
	|	Expression .*INIT*	
	|	true	
	|	false	
	|	¬ Predicate1	U
	|	Predicate1 ∧ Predicate1	L
	|	Predicate1 ∨ Predicate1	L
	|	Predicate1 ⇒ Predicate1	R
	|	Predicate1 ⇔ Predicate1	L
	|	(Predicate)	

Relation	::=	=	
	|	∈	
	|	Identifier	
	|	InfixRelationName	
LetDefinition	::=	VariableName == Expression	

6.8 Expressions

Expression0	::=	λ SchemaText • Expression	
	|	μ SchemaText • Expression	
	|	**let** LetDefinition ; ...; LetDefinition • Expression	
	|	Expression	
Expression	::=	**if** Predicate **then** Expression **else** Expression	
	|	Expression1	
Expression1	::=	Expression1 InfixGenericName Expression1	R
	|	Expression2 × Expression2 × ... × Expression2	
	|	Expression2	
Expression2	::=	Expression2 InfixFunctionName Expression2	L
	|	ℙ Expression4	
	|	PrefixGenericName Expression4	
	|	− Decoration Expression4	
	|	Expression4 ⦇ Expression0 ⦈ Decoration	
	|	Expression3	
Expression3	::=	Expression3 Expression4	
	|	Expression4	
Expression4	::=	VariableName *[*ActualParameters*]*	
	|	*self*	
	|	Number	
	|	SchemaReference	
	|	ClassName *[*ActualParameters*]* *[*RenameList*]*	
	|	↓ Expression4	
	|	Expression4 ∪ Expression4 ∪...∪ Expression4	L
	|	Expression4 ©	
	|	SetExpression	
	|	⟨ *[*Expression ,..., Expression*]* ⟩	
	|	⟦ *[*Expression ,..., Expression*]* ⟧	
	|	(Expression ,..., Expression)	
	|	θ SchemaName Decoration *[*Renamelist*]*	
	|	Expression4 . VariableName	

| Expression4 PostfixFunctionName
| Expression4^{Expression}
| (Expression0)

SetExpression ::= { [Expression , . . . , Expression] }
| { SchemaText [• Expression] }

VariableName ::= Identifier
| (OperatorName)

Identifier ::= Word Decoration

OperatorName ::= _ InfixFunctionName _
| InfixGenericName _
| InfixRelationName _
| PrefixGenericName _
| PrefixRelationName _
| _ PostfixFunctionName
| _(| _ |) Decoration
| _ Decoration

InfixFunctionName ::= InfixFunctionSymbol Decoration

InfixGenericName ::= InfixGenericSymbol Decoration

InfixRelationName ::= InfixRelationSymbol Decoration

PrefixGenericName ::= PrefixGenericSymbol Decoration

PrefixRelationName ::= PrefixRelationSymbol Decoration

PostfixFunctionName ::= PostfixFunctionSymbol Decoration

InfixFunctionSymbol ::= $\mapsto$ 1
| $..$ 2
| $+$ 3
| $-$ 3
| $\cup$ 3
| $\setminus$ 3
| $\frown$ 3
| $\uplus$ 3
| $\uminus$ 3
| $*$ 4
| div 4
| mod 4
| $\cap$ 4

	|	↿	4
	|	↾	4
	|	$⨾$	4
	|	$\circ$	4
	|	$\otimes$	4
	|	$\oplus$	5
	|	#	5
	|	$\lhd$	6
	|	$\rhd$	6
	|	⩤	6
	|	⩥	6
PostfixFunctionSymbol	::=	$\sim$	
	|	*	
	|	+	
InfixRelationSymbol	::=	$\neq$	
	|	$\notin$	
	|	$\subseteq$	
	|	$\subset$	
	|	$<$	
	|	$\leqslant$	
	|	$\geqslant$	
	|	$>$	
	|	prefix	
	|	suffix	
	|	in	
	|	⋿	
	|	$\sqsubseteq$	
	|	partition	
PrefixRelationSymbol	::=	disjoint	
InfixGenericSymbol	::=	$\leftrightarrow$	
	|	⇸	
	|	$\rightarrow$	
	|	⤔	
	|	$\rightarrowtail$	
	|	⤀	
	|	$\twoheadrightarrow$	
	|	⤖	
	|	⇻	
	|	⤕	
PrefixGenericSymbol	::=	$\mathbb{P}_1$	
	|	id	

	|	$\mathbb{F}$
	|	$\mathbb{F}_1$
	|	seq
	|	seq_1
	|	iseq
	|	bag
Decoration	::=	[Stroke ... Stroke]
Stroke	::=	′
	|	?
	|	!
	|	$_{\text{Number}}$
Word		Undecorated name or special symbol
Number		Unsigned decimal integer

Bibliography

Object Orientation

Booch, G. (1994) *Object-Oriented Analysis and Design with Applications*, Addison-Wesley.

Meyer, B. (1988 & 1997) *Object-Oriented Software Construction*, Prentice Hall.

Z

Hayes, I. (ed) (1987 & 1993) *Specification Case Studies*, Prentice Hall.

Potter, B., Sinclair, J. and Till, D. (1992) *An Introduction to Formal Specification and Z*, Prentice Hall.

Spivey, J.M. (1989 & 1992) *The Z Notation: A Reference Manual*, Prentice Hall. Available on-line at `http://spivey.oriel.ox.ac.uk/~mike/zrm/`.

Woodcock, J.C.P. and Davies, J. (1996) *Using Z: Specification, Refinement and Proof*, Prentice Hall.

Object Orientation and Z

Lano, K. and Haughton, H. (eds) (1994) *Object-Oriented Specification Case Studies*, Prentice Hall.

Stepney, S., Bardon, R. and Cooper, D. (eds) (1992) *Object Orientation in Z*, Prentice Hall.

Index